"It's less a book than a rumination, a prose poem, a Guthrie-esque howl of protest. . . . Clearly Vollmann is writing from his heart. He longs in earnest to get away from, or back to, America, and such longing lies at the core of our national literature."

—*New York Times Book Review*

"A writer whose books tower over the work of his contemporaries."

—*Washington Post Book World*

"Vollmann's lyric prose manages to convey both the velocity of train travel and the intensity of the sensual experience, a jolting achievement in an era of 'comfort travel' that has sought mostly to annihilate our relationship with the landscape."   —*Boston Globe*

"William T. Vollmann seeks fellowship in the quintessentially American subculture of boxcar-jumping hoboes in *Riding Toward Everywhere*."   —*Vanity Fair*

"Vollmann balances this idiosyncratic reporting with considerable literary references. . . . He considers Twain's revisit of the river he once piloted in *Life on the Mississippi*, wryly suggesting that contemporary train-hopping likewise represents an American pastime lost to abandoned memory."   —*Chicago Sun-Times*

"A labor of love. . . . Vollmann is always worth reading."

—*Seattle Times*

"William T. Vollmann writes impeccably researched works of fiction and nonfiction. . . . [He] ably renders, in writing as pungent as diesel fumes but a whole lot more bracing to absorb, the 'myriad reversals of fortune and feeling' that attend train-hopping [and which] bring him to life. . . . Vollmann's constituency is anyone interested in the written word's indelible ability to effect social change. . . . Prepare yourself . . . for the experience of having your cerebellum massaged in new and startling ways."

—*San Francisco Chronicle*

"A monster; monster talent, ambition, and accomplishment. . . . Vollmann still finds some juice in the conceit, so much so that his literary gift propels this slender, elegantly written book along like a third rail."   —*Los Angeles Times*

"An immense literary talent."   —*New York Times*

"The restless genius of prodigious writer William T. Vollmann is on electrifying display in *Riding Toward Everywhere* (Ecco), a gritty, gorgeous, and spirited travelogue of his train-hopping adventures out west with fellow 'fauxbo' Steve that chronicles the highs and lows of their risky, unforgettable days and 'diesel-scented' nights."

—*Elle*

"The brilliant, anarchistic writer William T. Vollmann [has written] a philosophical meditation on the boundaries of freedom and on the venerable American tradition. . . . In parts gloriously lyrical, in others thought-provoking . . . the book is worth reading because Vollmann is such a superb writer and because, in an age of irony, he is not afraid to speak with passionate intensity about the things that matter to him most."   —*St. Louis Post-Dispatch*

William T. Vollmann

About the Author

WILLIAM T. VOLLMANN is the author of seven novels; three collections of stories; a seven-volume critique of violence, *Rising Up and Rising Down*; and *Poor People*, an examination of poverty around the globe. His most recent novel, *Europe Central*, won the National Book Award, and he has also won the PEN Center USA West Award for Fiction and the Whiting Writers' Award. His journalism and fiction have been published in the *New Yorker*, *Esquire*, *Spin*, and *Granta*. Vollmann lives in Sacramento with his wife and child.

ALSO BY WILLIAM T. VOLLMANN

* Published by Ecco

RIDING TOWARD
EVERYWHERE

WILLIAM T. VOLLMANN

AN ecco BOOK

HARPER PERENNIAL

NEW YORK • LONDON • TORONTO • SYDNEY • NEW DELHI • AUCKLAND

HARPER ● PERENNIAL

FIRST HARPER PERENNIAL EDITION PUBLISHED 2009.

Designed by Cassandra J. Pappas

The Library of Congress has catalogued the hardcover edition as follows:

Vollmann, William T.
    Riding toward everywhere / by William T. Vollmann.—1st ed.
      p. cm.
      ISBN 978-0-06-125675-2
    1. Vollmann, William T.—Travel.   2. Railroad travel.   I. Title.
    PS3572.O395Z46   2008
    818'.5403—dc22   2007031551

ISBN 978-0-06-125676-9 (pbk.)

09 10 11 12 13 WBC/RRD 10 9 8 7 6 5 4 3 2 1

This book is dedicated to STEVE JONES,

who never pretended

that he or I were hobos

and who therefore coined the word fauxbeaux,

who turned fifty riding the rails with me,

who was riding the rails with me as I turned forty-seven,

who never made me feel guilty for saying

that this or that train was too fast for me,

and who is the finest Christian

who ever bought me a cigar,

drank my booze

or shouted fuck!

into the diesel-scented night.

They said they would rather be outlaws a year in Sherwood Forest than President of the United States forever.

MARK TWAIN, *Tom Sawyer* (1876)

LEGAL DISCLAIMER

I have never been caught riding on a freight train. So let's say I have never committed misdemeanor trespass. The stories in this book are all hearsay, and the photographs are really drawings done in steel-grey crayon. None of the individuals depicted are any more real than I. Moreover, trainhopping may harm or kill you. Finally, please consider yourself warned that the activities described in this book are criminally American.

TEMPORAL DISCLAIMER

This book was written at a time of extreme national politics. These circumstances shaped my thoughts about riding trains in specific ways described below. Accordingly, I have left all references to the currrent administration in the present tense. As the Russians would say, *he who has ears will hear.*

WTV
2005–2006

CONTENTS

RIDING TOWARD
EVERYWHERE

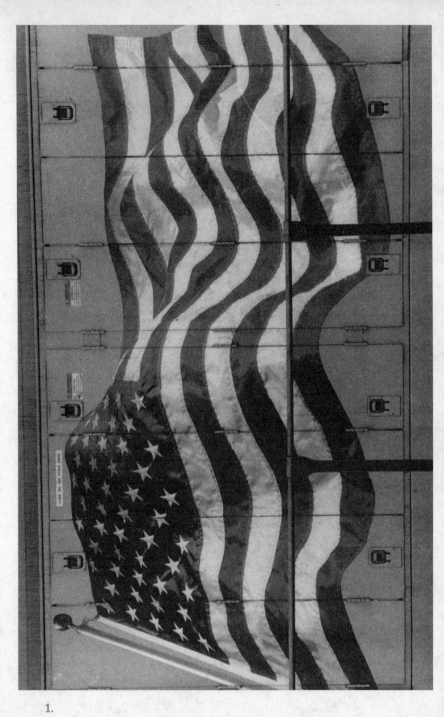

1.

A SHORT ESSAY ON FREIGHT TRAINS

1.

I **am my** father's son. On a recent Christmas, in the bakery which not only is the best in town but never forgets it, we were waiting to pick up our pie, and my father came to my side to chat with me. One of the highest sugar-and-butter arbiters, who puts the public in its place even in seasons when it cannot overwhelm her, commanded: *Sir,* you need to stop blocking the line *right now!*—My father turned to me and remarked conversationally: Give some people a little power and they turn into Nazis, don't they?

My father grew up in an era when to be an American—a white American, at least—was to be yourself. In some respects his generation was more ignorant, complacent, self-centered and parochial than mine. For better and for worse, it actually believed in progress, which is to say that it was also more sure of itself, comparatively self-reliant and accordingly less corrupted by toadying—more *American* in the best sense. My grandfather's time must have been even more individualistic. With his by-Gods and goddamns, my grandfather laid down opinions without great reverence for the judgments of others. —I just don't know, Bill, he said once at a museum exhibit on the history of female suffrage. Maybe we shouldn't have given women the vote. What do you think? —And he got his reward: glares of hatred and outrage from all ladies present. —Does contrarianism equal freedom of thought? I prefer my grandfather's abrasive and frequently tedious self-assertion to my neighbors' equivalently wrongheaded chorus. But should I label him any the less conformist? He once told me that if I had been his son he would have beaten my differentness out of me. It was his faith that American authority could do no wrong, in evidence of which I quote one of his pronouncements: You know what burns me up? All those rioters complaining about the police trampling on their *rights*! Don't they get it? When there's a riot, those sons of bitches have no rights! —As for my father, his epoch was the heyday of the Organization Man, and he respected rules, hierarchies and technocratic methods more than he knew; he simply happened to be good enough to make some of the rules. I once asked him why he wore a suit every working day, and he replied that one picks one's battles and he had more interesting battles to fight than dress code skirmishes. He was right. When I need to meet somebody important in Japan, I wear my suit. It is probable that my father enjoys his suits more than I do. In any event, fortified by them he looked factory managers in the eye and told them exactly where they were screwing up. —Weren't you just a little hard on those guys? an Associate Vice-President inquired—an accolade my father reported with glee. He taught his students without fear or favor, never missing a lecture in all the decades of his career. He worked hard, lived the life he chose, and said precisely what he thought. On his desk lay a paperweight engraved with his favorite motto: BULLSHIT BAFFLES BRAINS.

I am my father's son, which is to say that I am not exactly my father. In some ways I am shyer than he, in others more extreme and bold. My father believes that drugs should be legalized, regulated and taxed. So do I. My father has never sampled a controlled substance and never will. I've proudly committed every victimless crime that I can think of. My father actively does not want to know which acts I have performed and with whom.

I still go to the bakery my father hates, and the woman who told my father to get back in line nods at me. My father will never go back there. Perhaps if I were more my father's son I wouldn't patronize the place, either. But I am less proud than he, more submissive—or maybe more indifferent.

I work hard, make money, not as effectively as my father did but well enough to get by. I say what I think, and sometimes get a reward surpassing my grandfather's: death threats. So far, I've never missed a deadline for a term paper, a review, a manuscript. I perform the mumbo-jumbo of voting with belief in my heart, I've not yet won even a jaywalking ticket, and unlike my father, whom I fault in this respect, I refrain from opting out of jury duty; instead, they mostly kick me out.

My father hates organized religion, probably because he hates the God who killed his little girl back in 1968. I find religions variously bemusing. My father likes nice cars and is a sucker for the latest gadget. I enjoy the few mechanical devices which are simple enough for me to understand, such as semiautomatic pistols. My father hunted in his youth and still occasionally shoots handguns with me, but has come to disapprove of civilian firearms ownership, an attitude which disappoints me. He has voted Republican most of his life, but he and I agree in hating the current President.

My father has lived in Europe for many years. I am not sure that he realizes how much his native country has changed. People don't dare anymore to talk back the way he used to.

As I get older, I find myself getting angrier and angrier. Doubtless change itself, not to mention physical decline and inevitable petty tragedies of disappointed expectations, would have made for resentment in any event; but I used to be a passive schoolboy, my negative impulses turned obediently inward. Now I gaze around this increasingly un-American America of mine, and I rage.

So many of these developments are well-meaning. Children must buckle up in the school buses, and, speaking of children, I had better not enter into conversation with a child I don't know, in case the parents brand me a molester. On that same subject, a schoolboy has sex with his teacher, gets her pregnant, and off she goes to prison! The safety announcements on airplanes get not only longer, but louder and more authoritarian. (Rousseau, 1754: *It is thus with man . . . as he becomes sociable and a slave, he grows weak, timid and servile . . . his effeminate way of life totally enervates his strength and courage.*) My city passes an ordinance to confiscate the cars of men who pick up prostitutes. That compels me to walk. Whenever I check into a motel with my own companion of the evening, the clerk requires an identification card. Many of these establishments reject my business nowadays, because I lack a credit card. A two-hundred-dollar deposit or even five hundred for a forty-dollar room will not persuade them to take a chance on me. The few who do insist on photocopying my identification. Should I leave the country with a large wad of cash on my person, it is incumbent on me to report it. What *don't* I have to report, and what happens to the information which I so dutifully give?

Year by year, those good Germans march deeper into my life. I have been interrogated by the FBI twice now, and by the U.S. Customs and Immigration functionaries more times than I can remember. The FBI have always been polite, although I would hardly call them warm. Their colleagues in other branches of authority have occasionally intimidated, insulted and detained me. I used to be with a woman who would plead with me to *play the game a little*; I was doing this to myself, she said. But I figured that they were doing it to me.

I am my father's son. I stare back into their eyes. Once upon a time, a Customs bully who had already held my underwear high in the air for the delectation of people in line behind me dumped every carefully packed item out of my suitcase, tore the wrappers off my presents, brought his face close to mine and said: You know what? I'm just getting warmed up. —Oh, officer, I replied, if only I'd saved some of those *neat little green* pills for you to find. You know, those *cute little green happy pills.* —And I kept smiling and staring into the creep's face.

My father, I am sorry to say, now believes that I should cool it. (I've told you that he and I both hate the President. But I would like to see the President in prison.) It may well be that I am a sullen and truculent citizen; possibly I should *play the game* a trifle. But I do, I do: When I pick up prostitutes I use somebody else's car.

2.

My critique of American society remains fundamentally incoherent. Would I really have preferred my grandfather's time, when Pinkertons were cracking Wobblies over the head, or my father's, when Joe McCarthy could ruin anyone by calling him Red? All I know is that although I live a freer life than many people, I want to be freer still; I'm sometimes positively dazzled with longing for a better way of being. What is it that I need?

3.

What do you need? asked the woman in the bushes.

To catch out.

No, what do you *need*?

The other bush people waved me away, not threateningly but urgently. They were accomplishing crystal deals; oh, yes; they were buying and selling the Big Rock Candy Mountain. Nobody would tell where the freight trains stopped.

So we went south along the rails, the three of us, all the way to the overpass from whose exalted edge we hoped to see the telltale double track, and we entered the graffiti'd warren beneath. Like most experiments, this became a cul-de-sac; but the cyclone fence enclosing us daunted only me: my pelvis, recently healed of a fracture, still ached in bad weather. I stayed there with my ridiculous orange bucket, listening to truck-thuds upon the concrete over my head while my fitter friends climbed up and over. They never said a word to make me feel ashamed. Nor did I feel downcast or beholden; for among the equipment of us adventurers who've ridden the iron horse bareback, so to speak—the seat one finds on a freightcar is scarcely gifted with overmuch padding—is very commonly to be found my father's three best qualities: courage, generosity and integrity. I sat on my orange bucket, and my friends came back saying they'd found no spoor of any train.

So we walked back to the passenger station of Salinas, California. I had been useless beneath the overpass, but I was the one who spied our train through an alley! We ran, then circumspectly walked down the yard, passing a woman who was fellating a man on the gravel. Moments after we rounded the tail of the snake, the hissing of compressed air warned us that it was about to slither off the edge of the world. We leaped on just in time, or rather my friends did; I employed my risible orange bucket, which I upended, stood on, and then after stepping easily up from onto the train pulled it after me by means of a string attached to the handle; I was my father's son; I liked my gadgets. —*Hey!* somebody had kidded me when we were walking down the tracks. *You stole my bucket! Gimme back my orange bucket!* —An orange bucket was not such a bad thing, aside from the fact that it was orange. One could sit on it, carry things in it and piss into it. I sat on it and looked around.

We were riding a lumber gondola whose huge packets of planks bore one rectangular gap on the righthand side, another smaller gap on the left, and a passage between them. It was the perfect refuge; we could dodge the bulls no matter which side they chose. Hunkering down against officialdom, we passed through the yard at increasing speed, reached and left that former overpass in a couple of breaths, and off we sped, accompanied by fog, mountains and waterlined fields, with the dim dusk scrolling by, the train shuddering and groaning, the wood groaning. Our hope was Santa Barbara.

Departing a yard always feels to me somewhat like crossing a bridge over a deep gorge; one commits oneself to someone else's defense against the void. By the time the signal has fallen behind, and many tracks have gone to one, the freight's velocity is usually too great for the rider to do anything but ride. In short: Next stop Santa Barbara, always assuming that we stop in Santa Barbara—

I had never ridden among lumber-stacks before and was apprehensive that they might shift. Eventually I consoled myself with the thought that if they did slam together, I would likely die instantly, so there was nothing to fear. Moreover, Steve, who is the hero of this book, had ridden gondolas many times and seemed unworried, so I let it go, relishing the open air and the smell of fresh lumber around me.*

That was the great thing about this sort of ride: breathing the air of reality. In the Gilroy country the evening smelled of garlic; later on, near Santa Barbara, the dawn would smell of anise. Freight train rides are parables. Why have we chosen to live behind walls and windows? For an answer, feel the shocking blackness and feeling of asphyxiation when a freight train enters a tunnel! An old man once told me about riding a freight in some nebulous northern realm where a tunnel was so long that the hobo on top of the gondola fell off dead; the old man succeeded in becoming an old man because he rode in a boxcar full of air! Was that a tall tale? I don't know.† But I can assure you that the tunnel-darkness beyond the window of a subway car or passenger car, however eerie it might be, is quite innocuus compared to the *real* blackness that wrenches breath away. Reality caresses and stings! For a fact, reality kills; so does reality denied; at least when reality lays hands on me I *feel* it. I never want not to feel.

But the peculiarity was that our train was so loud that the vibrations of the diagonal cables holding the lumber-stacks to the center beam could be perceived only by touch, not through the ears. So that aspect of my experience was not entirely real, either, which confused and bemused me; because just as outside is more

*When Steve's secret agent in the Union Pacific, a locomotive engineer, read this chapter, he was horrified and made Steve promise never to ride a lumber gondola again. Apparently the wood can indeed shift when a freight brakes.

†One freight rider believes that hobos did used to suffocate *in the days of steam.* He lists America's three longest freight tunnels: Libby Dam (eight miles), Cascade (almost eight miles) and Moffat (six miles). I hope never to pass through any of them.

real than inside, and the freight train experience of outside perceived at high speeds is more real still, so it seems only right that *every* sensation should expand; the fact that one of reality's fundamental characteristics is *constraint* is something that freight riding seduces me into denying whenever I can. On the iron horse I experience the state of unlimited expansion.

We rushed on. A flare of evening sun in the Gabilan Range (pink chalcedony), the white loveliness of rainbirds blowing spray in elongated flower petals, the Sierra de Salinas to the west, the leaden darkness of a lettuce field, all these perceptions granted to me right next to the freeway became my loveliest treasures which I hope to hoard right up to the cemetery lights amidst the last golden-green of the fields.

At dusk the train halted alongside a dingy white wall whose graffiti had been whitewashed into irregular shapes of a different griminess, and on the far side of that wall and its weeds, a beautiful young Latina stood holding her daughter's hand and gazing at the train. I waved to them, and they smiled and waved back. The loneliness went away from me, and even now I feel gladdened by the memory of that moment. After a time their men came out. They too stood and waved. I never called a word to them, but I will remember them forever.

Into the dark went the train now, accompanied by few and pale lights and by more darkness which compressed the already flattened ground. I inhaled the darkness of vegetation and pallid darknesses of fields, the corpse-white dirt roads, everything glimpsed between stacks of lumber, in the cut between high ridges of darkness. Halfway up my lumber-stack I suddenly spied the lemony-yellow lights of a small ranch and wondered what it would be like to live there for the rest of my life. Like the lumber piles shifting subtly back and forth, neither solid enough to be entirely safe nor sufficiently yield-ing not to crush me, the lives I could have lived or at least imagined living teased me; in two steps I could have leaped off the rusty metal trainbed and made landfall in sight of that ranch; then I would have lived out my life there in truth, for my speed would have killed me. But nothing felt inimical, except occasionally those lashed-down towers of Canadian Douglas fir around me—and when I say *me* this is not to deny the presence of my two compan-ions, with whom I shared my pleasures in common; but just as a family can go to church together and sit side by side on the pew while experiencing (or not) separate communions with the many-faced Spirit, so I, for whom "organized religion" is useless, and like-wise my friends, although we shared food, water, booze, cigars and vigilance, remained gloriously alone in that nightscape. I saw a tall palm silhouetted in the night, then a tall forest. I saw it, and then it was gone. How could I know what my companions saw? Why shout my perceptions into their ears? The Greeks prized a substance called *electrum,* a mixture of silver and gold. I gazed upward, and thought: *the pure electrum color of the moon.*

Slowly chewing a date, wrapped up in all my jackets, I stretched out on bare steel which was truly a luxurious bed thanks to the soft, soft shadow of the darkness; and my friends were asleep when I rode the trestle bridge's black shadow on the silver river. I rode it through the smell of river and grass, and a bright star in the sky kept me company, turning bluish-white for my delight until a sudden invasion of road lights drowned it in alien bright-ness. Happily, those excrescences fell behind quickly. My star returned to me. The moon was playing hide and seek with the ridge, then came a canyon with moon-white grass and trees as richly leaved as thunderheads, the night sky almost white by comparison; and I hope never to see this place by day because it was so perfect in its night-incarnation, being not merely my past but the vanished American West itself where I would have home-steaded with my pioneer bride; I would have planted orchards and drunk from the artesian well of dreams.

Leaning up against the lumber whose undulations lulled me into the illusion that this great mass felt friendly toward me, I found that my ears could finally make out the tight humming of those double cables, and my eyes grew ever more sensitive in the darkness. But suddenly we approached the freeway, sad canal of false light amidst the grass, and my sight got scorched back down to normalcy . . .

Whenever we stopped, Steve jumped down with great energy, rushing up and down the train; once it started moving and he could hardly see where he had come from in the darkness but Brian and I pulled him back up; on another occasion he was prowling in the gravel when authority came with a flashlight and we froze. Authority missed us; we clicketyclacked away into our dreams.

4.

Speaking of authority, the Vandenberg Air Force Base, through whose domain we now passed, was off limits to civilians, and therefore delightfully roadless in stretches. Thanks to author-ity, this place was sequestered, and so we saw dolphins leaping beneath the moon.

5.

After a night which lasted for a pleasant and chilly year, it was finally almost dawn, the milky blue Pacific lying just right of the train, it seemed, and a single milky-yellow light fixed itself in the water as unvaryingly as the moon. I thought that it must be some very distant Coast Guard beacon. A single white diagonal of wave-crest lay motionless across the ocean. Then the air brightened, and all the other waves burst into view with their related motions. The sea air remained humid and cold, my hands chilly but not numb; the coldest part of me was my feet in their damp socks.

Here came a lovely long black islet . . .

(When I read this over, the pallidity of my descriptions appalls me, as if I had failed to make what I saw "real" enough. This must be the product of my velocity, which prevented me from seeing more than the things themselves. One scans an islet, and it is complete and therefore perfect; then it is gone.)

The freight kept going right through Santa Barbara, and we thought we might have to ride to Ventura or beyond, but just south of Carpinteria it slowed, and what increased our motivation to get off just then was that a man with a walkie-talkie was standing in the gravel, staring into each car, and his eyes met mine, at which point he raised the walkie-talkie to his mouth. The train kept travelling southward at about the same speed as a running man, so when the walkie-talkie man was the merest dot behind us we jumped out, landing either erect or on our hands and knees as we thought best. Then we began to walk away from that life. It was half-past seven in the morning. Crossing the highway, we regrouped against the wall of a gated community, and Steve called his daughter on a cell phone while I pissed on a tree.

We started to walk. There was a street, then a sealed culvert which made us backtrack and take another road. After a couple of miles we reached the Pacific. My good and patient friends waited for me without recriminations while I toiled over a breakwater's boulders, anxious not to crack my pelvis again. A series of small strokes had wrecked my balance, and what would have taken them fifteen minutes took me an hour. I remember this part of the journey with nearly as much pleasure as the rest, a fact for which I must credit my companions' forbearance. It is a fine luxury to trust oneself to a friend's strengths and help him in his weaknesses, all without negotiations or resentments. Steve and I share this. Brian, whom I know less, offers a similarly gentle understanding. My doctor had told me not to ride any freight trains, but I never worried that these two men would be put out even if I inconvenienced them.

We arrived at a terraced southern California restaurant, where in spite of our grubbiness the waiters gave us free coffee; they looked Mexican; perhaps they pitied us because so many of their people had crossed the desert in attempts to come here, and so many of the ones who succeeded then got arrested or otherwise turned away. Steve's wife and daughter came to get us, and we all went out for breakfast, we three men eating hugely. Then the ladies went shopping, and we slept the afternoon in Steve's daughter's apartment, I on the floor, Brian on the couch, Steve upstairs in the bed. It was one of my favorite happy and delicious sleeps; and when I awoke it was a great pleasure to lie a moment longer on the soft carpet, safe from reality. Indeed, the entire apartment felt soft, clean and voluptuously warm, with little possibility of interference from men with walkie-talkies. Ordinarily it would have bored me. As it was, I loved it gratefully. What could be better than resting here? Sometimes after a long day I lie back on my bed, with the covers up to my waist, watching my little girl nestle on the floor with her toy rabbit and her two toy pandas, and it is so wonderful to watch her and think nothing. I ask her what she is thinking and she says: I think that I don't know what I am thinking. —This was how it was for me at Steve's daughter's apartment. I could happily have gone back to sleep. But Steve and Brian were on the porch smoking cigars. I went out and they shared beers with me.

It was Steve's fiftieth birthday. Brian and I took him out for dinner at an Italian restaurant. Then we all returned to sleep.

On the next morning we took the Amtrak first from Santa Barbara to Goleta, then, when we saw no double track, changed our minds and stayed on the train, buying new tickets for San Luis Obispo. In silence, the conductor admired my orange bucket. It was a comfortably innocuous ride alongside the blue and whitish-blue plain of sea, an extraordinarily flat sea with greenish-white traceries. The gulls on the tan beach were now accompanied by a fleet of red kayaks. The palm trees, dome tents and pretty beach girls were no longer the world as they had been when I had seen them from the lumber gondola, but a series of pictures bordered by window-sills. I cannot say that they were better or worse. We ordered beers from the dining car and luxuriously drank them. Once again I saw schools of porpoises. At about one-fifteen we arrived in San Luis Obispo.

One always hides when one's freight enters a yard. I remember how from my rathole between lumber-piles two nights before I'd observed the sinister illumination of this very station alone and cautiously as my friends snored. It had then seemed as daunting as an enemy military installation. Now it was a harmless afternoon place, open to the public, because we were there legally. It was high time for that legality to end.

Discreetly paralleling the train yard on the nearest street, we walked northward for a block or two, then rejoined the tracks out of sight of the station. There was no litter here, unfortunately; this must not be a spot which had brought good luck to our vagrant colleagues. And south of the station we'd seen a large track crew. It seemed best to lie low for awhile. My more agile companions went over the fence and I slithered under it, my oilskin pants getting good and muddy, and down we all ducked into the creekside's poison oak and up the other bank, up the steep eucalyptus hill to the parking lot where a girl on a bicycle told us that one locked-looking gate wasn't really locked, and it wasn't, so we went down the hill and ran across the clearing which was bordered on one side by a fenced house with a **NO TRESPASSING** sign and on the other by the tracks themselves, from which we were screened by a narrow oasis of eucalyptus, geranium and palm. There we lurked like rodents, watching the tracks in the sun, framed by brightly graveled whiteness, rusty rails and birdsong. I felt edgy whenever a pickup door slammed on the tracks; what if that pickup belonged to someone with the authority to remove us? Next came the sound of a woodpecker, and engine noises far and close. We were not so much *hopeful* as *ready*.

Brian and I took a stroll to see whether we might best relocate, for I worried that the head of the train might stop so close to our hiding place that the conductor would see. So we ascended the overpass and gazed north and south along the tracks all the way to Everywhere. In the end we knew as much as we had before.

When we returned down into the world, we saw two truckloads of workers on the open side of the trees; they were staring and pointing at us, so we wandered around the corner and checked with Steve on his cellphone. He was hugging the ground. We strolled down to the liquor store and got some beers. After an hour, the train men finally left. We brought Steve his beer, which was still relatively cold, and then stretched out in the grass, waiting for our train. It was the waiting that Steve most hated about this sport. I myself had always been better at that than at boarding moving trains; to each his own. More hours went by, as empty as the tracks themselves.

Steve was listening to music through his headphones; Brian was staring at the sky. Peering through the bushes, I saw the same vacant tracks as ever. So I wandered down to the Amtrak office and asked at the counter when the next passenger train was coming. The clerk informed me that there was track trouble to the south. That meant we had time for dinner. We walked into a diner, flirted with the waitress, who liked Brian best and me worst, and wolfed down our sandwiches. No train came. Lying in the pine needles, we breathed the honeyed hours of illegal time. I argued that we should lurk near the overpass, so that we could board a long train near the rear without being seen; but my companions pointed out with good reason that the oasis where we had spent the afternoon, and indeed that entire east side of the tracks, was less exposed. So I was outvoted.

When night came, Steve saw a locomotive with an open door and proposed that we hide in there, but as soon as we'd entered its darkness a light came on across the tracks and Brian was sure that we'd been seen, so we ran back down and along the righthand side of the tracks, hoping to reach our oasis, but by the time we've reached the shed, here came a man with a giant flashlight! Another Amtrak was coming south, its lights aimed at us. The conductor dismounted. Brian and I froze against the shadowiest wall of the shed; Steve had already gone. The man approached and shone his light; I was sure that he saw me, but he did nothing. He was a steward; he locked the gates to some of the tracks. As soon as he was gone, we threw ourselves down in the grass.

The Amtrak tolled its bell and hauled its two tiers of yellow windows down the tracks to bed, hissing and snoring in front of us for a long time.

Suddenly the conductor was walking toward us down the gravel; my heart was pounding. Officials with flashlights came straight toward us . . .

Trust me, said Steve. Their eyes aren't adjusted. They can't see us.

He was right. I experienced a surprisingly extreme fear, commingled with the fascination of observing a rare phenonemon: namely, our own supernatural power of invisibility. These men in uniform, I could almost have touched their ankles! They were so close now that their various yellow probes of wrist-light puddled around them and caught the grass around my elbows. They were islands of authority in the night, with immense theoretical power over us, but, like us, they were small and alone; the night was huger than any of us. And we were more a part of the night than they. This was their property, their station, and we were trespassing on it but they could not see us. When they turned and went back indoors, I felt almost as if I could fly.

We crouched in the poison oak. Then a dog barked, a light came on, and the homeowner coughed a few feet away. We froze, and instead of believing I was an eagle I longed to be an earthworm. And here came more functionaries with flashlights.

That last gate . . . one of them said.

That was our gate. Steve and I ran up the hill as fast as we could and threw ourselves down into the leaves. But this time the man with the flashlight saw Steve's pack and my cursed orange bucket.

Someone's HIDIN', he chuckled like a wicked giant in a fairytale.

In a fright, we ran into the weeds and clung together like lovers. The man shone his flashlight directly on us. But we were in the shadows and our clothing was dark. Perhaps he didn't see us. We waited through the pale white lights, the blinking blue light on the track, the yellow light through the palm fronds, and we spied on the rusty tracks which were now milk-silver in the security lights. Again menacing silhouettes with caps and flashlights advanced upon us, and our hearts pounded. They shone their lights in our faces, but once again failed to catch us. A century later the track steward returned, locked the gates to the Amtrak, and retreated into his place behind the dark window, then transformed himself into a mannequin and stood there forever and a day; probably what we took to be him was a wooden post or something. Life was the whish of air, the rustle of grass, and I hoped I was not still lying in poison oak.

Now it was midnight and our freight finally arrived, but on the far side of a passenger train.

Shit, shit, said Steve. Bill, you were right . . .

A crew swarmed around the passenger train, which was southbound. A man's voice said: There's a freight ahead of us. It's a-goin' over the hill to Oakland . . .

I abandoned my orange bucket. We ran right acrosss the head of the train, and the engineer either failed to see us or else out of pity or indifference refrained from reporting us. So, having rounded our next chapter's dangerous beginning, we slowed into facsimiles of law-abiding citizens and strolled down the west side of the tracks and into the darkness, passing through the parking lot on the side of the station. Then we were there: the stopped freight stretched infinitely southward.

At this particular phase of the sport, I am always in a tearing hurry, for who knows when the train will start? Steve, whose agility and speed are superior to mine, is blasé. He wouldn't mind standing there while the train begins to move, for he feels entirely ready to seize an appropriate ladder as it pulls past. Not I.

So for my own sake I urged my friends to hasten, and they

obliged me. Soon enough we met the darkness of an open boxcar. Steve, who hated boxcars, wanted to look for something better, but we'd gone only a few cars farther south when the brakes began to hiss. I persuaded the other two to come back, and while they tapped the door open with a railroad spike I wriggled up and in, as proud of doing this without my bucket as a toddler is of walking; then I flicked on my flashlight just for a moment, to make sure that there was no excrement or broken glass, and saw graffiti of a naked woman's ass and a white, rather friendly skull on the white walls.

There came another hiss of air, and after ten hours of *hidin'* in San Luis Obispo the freight began to move; we'd been on board for perhaps a minute. And through the wide open door I saw a vast square wall of vivid life!

All the waiting, that living fieldmouse-small in the grass, was a necessary part of our experience, because it transformed motion into salvation. When I hitchhike, I experience the same feeling. And I wonder whether life can be good without the hard times.

Tree-silhouettes against white sky, pallid sky, dim grass, house-lights, the tremendous clatter of existence, these things brought me happiness as crystal-clear as a vegetarian girl's urine. There came a brief stop on a trestle high above a night freeway, and it was like a lovely picture in a gallery.

Now my life went on in the smell of metal, dirt and old paint; and the skull smiled jawlessly upon me from the white wall. My flashlight discovered a tagline from La Grande, Oregon, a place with bittersweet associations for me. I had been there more than once with a woman whom I had deeply loved. She was the one who had thought it served me right to be punished by authority for failing to *play the game a little*. We left each other over that and other things. But how I'd loved her! There she was, written on the wall which carried me through an infinity of other lives; and if I chose, I could go back to her, or at least beg her . . . I was riding through my dreams again. How long would it take to get to Oregon on the freights? Three days, maybe. She and I had walked the tracks of the Portland yard until a bull caught us; it hadn't been far from her house. I could easily get to her front door on foot . . . That was the journey I truly believed I could make, the journey into the past. It wouldn't do me any good to go to her now. I had to go to her in the time when she'd loved me. But I could, because riding the rails is time travel.

Dark and lovely tree-shadows raced across the long white gallery, and the shadows of my two comrades continually glided toward me, getting devoured by the pursuing shadow of the doorframe. Then all of the sudden, red signal-luminescence rushed into the boxcar and flushed us with the blood of the entire world!

6.

Freight trains remind me of my father's tools, and of those of both grandfathers, the one I've known and the one I hardly knew; both were machinists. My father's tools are heavy. They are more metal than plastic. The power tools sport cords as thick as promises. The tools of my grandfathers, the solid old micrometers and files, do not have anything to do with plastic or electricity. They are solid metal, knurled and dense. As for my father's tools, they are poxed with rust. When I inspect them, I worry that I might have been a bad son. I took care of them as well as I knew how, but did I "fail" or would even the canniest garage warrior have been defeated by now by time? While writing this essay, I finally threw away my father's power planer, whose rusty bed wobbled so dangerously when I fingered the switch that I feared it might whirl apart in my hands. When I ride the rails, I experience the same rusty shuddering of bare metal. I am going back to the time when my father's tools were new. Present realities fall away faster and faster. They cannot stop me any more than the flashlights of functionaries.

Indeed, that night the boxcar seemed to be speeding upward like a rocket under attack from anti-rocket missiles; it roared at what felt to be an ever increasing velocity, took evasive action by shaking from side to side and every now and then lurched horribly, as if it had just been hit. Sometimes I would be awakened from a light doze by the boxcar's sudden slamming, as if there had been an accident. Amidst all this shrieking and creaking, the immense open door amazed me, first exposing me to myself in the lighted city of the men's prison immediately to the west, then offering multitudes of foggy pictures all the way to dawn; I felt as if every possibility were offering itself through the doorway, but without Mephisophelean trickery. The infinities available to me paraded as beguilingly as clock-figures on a medieval church tower. Before I knew it, I was asleep again, dreaming over choices I had been too sensible or cowardly to make.

My loyal friends woke me up because we were coming into Salinas! I leaped up, fully clothed and shoed like a soldier, slung my pack to my shoulder and was ready! But the train kept going. My friends stood dismayed.

Well, it was nice while it lasted, I said, and went back to sleep.

Six hours later the boxcar was still speeding and roaring toward Everywhere. We glimpsed cornfields and then the half-constructed houses of our ever-swarming California. It was a dirty sort of day. Just as a river glimpsed between the girders of a trestle bridge may decay into ordinariness when one actually goes swimming in it, so a landscape, particularly one maimed by human beings, will often be reduced by light to the merest concatenation of stunted or even poisonous possibilities. Although the boxcar was still, objectively speaking, huge, now that all the obscene drawings could be seen from one end to the other, our travelling gallery seemed to have shrunk; its grimy, rusty floor had grown drearier, and even the fabulous rectangle of real life projected upon its open movie screen was less enchanting, in part because most California cities are ugly, in part because I had hardly slept, and surely in some measure because riding the rails, like any attempt to escape from life, must taste of failure every now and then unless one is willing to die.

Presently we found ourselves highballing into Hayward and right through the yard, far too quickly for even Steve to consider getting off, then increasing velocity once again, and finally rolling into the Oakland yard with its multitudinous tracks, fences and walls and its stench of excrement; a baleful place which I would not wish to lurk in at night. Passing through Jack London Square, the train slowed to fifteen or twenty miles an hour, but by now we were already in Emeryville with the blue giraffes of container shipping cranes ahead; my friends feared that the train would not stop here, either, so we decided to jump off by a vote of two to one, I voting against. (Only I had thought to bring a wide-mouthed bottle to piss in. My friends were too respectful of railroad property to piss in the boxcar and might perhaps have been getting needy.) I was fearful, I admit; I have always avoided jumping on or off moving trains, even our disembarkation at Carpinteria the previous day had been for me a somewhat anxious affair; but there was nothing for it. Brian went first, fell, hit his head and slammed his hand against his bloody face, falling far behind us now. We couldn't leave him, so now we were all the more compelled to repeat his performance. Steve went next and landed erect, tough and bold on this first morning after his fiftieth birthday, but later admitted to having hurt his ankle. I, solicitous for my knees and pelvis, landed in a ball on the gravel, twisting my knee. I limped well enough; we all slithered under the yard's fence quite adequately; later I spent a day or two in bed with my leg on pillows.

7.

Whenever I injure or tire myself on the rails, I can rest, whether at home or in a flophouse. Although I won't own a cellphone myself, how sweet it was in San Luis Obispo to stroll around the bend, out of the railroad workers' sight, and then confer with Steve, who hugged the ground, murmuring through his cellphone into Brian's cell phone, so that we could plan our trespasses with scant risk or interference. Above all, how luxurious it is to travel I care not where for no good reason! As my best friend Ben likes to say, *What you get is what you get.* And I hope that as what I get diminishes, thanks to old age, erotic rejection, financial loss or authority's love-taps, I will continue to receive it gratefully. But there is no gainsaying the fact that what I've gotten is more than many people's share. Contempt for my privileged railroad follies may or may not be warranted. The question is what I make of them. When Thoreau went to ground at Walden Pond, he got the free use of Emerson's land. When he was jailed for refusing to pay his poll tax, a lady bailed him out. Do these two footnotes of dependency vitiate the integrity of his eloquence? It may well be that Thoreau lacked gratitude for these favors, or that his self-reliance was never as perfect as he pretended or I once imagined. What of that? During the time of their fashioning, words may or may not dwell with their maker in a relationship of "sincerity." After the maker has finished with them, they live to the extent that they inspire *us*. I might not have been allowed to be, nor wanted to be, Thoreau's friend. But *Walden* gives me pleasure and makes me braver. So does riding the rails. If this essay can do the same for you, then my material comforts, even if in your eyes they render me a dilettante or a hypocrite, have been useful means to that end. If this essay fails, the fault must be in it, in you, me, the orange bucket or some combination of the above; all the same, it was still written "sincerely."

8,

Well, you know what back child support is? the hobo at the side of the freeway said. Sixty-five percent of my check goes to that. I got an ex-wife that wants me to sign my kids away and I won't do it. It's a power trip on her part. My son, he still wants to keep my name, and it bugs her. So she says to me, *fine, your next stop's the streets.*

How long have you been on the road? I asked him.

Since '86. See, I was a boilermaker. I made twenty-two bucks an hour. Back in the seventies there was a big shortage of powerhouses. Well, the EPA jumped in and made it so hard to build 'em, that now they just repair 'em. And my ex-wife hit me with more than nine hundred a month for the two kids. Then President Clinton signed a bill so that every employer has to run your social security number through the computer within twenty-four hours, so if I work I get busted on the first check. I was filing married. If I'd filed single, I literally would have ended up owing money after a day's work.

Did you ever ride the rails?

Yeah. I rode the freights. Shitty. Like just plain dirty. When Burlington Northern and Santa Fe merged, they tightened all the screws. They see you, you go straight to jail. Right now I just hitchhike. I'm stranded here. Maybe I'll clear seven or eight bucks a day here. When I left Seattle I only had twenty and that wasn't enough. I wanna make at least fifty-sixty bucks here before I hit the next town . . .

I talked with that hobo awhile. Then I gave him money, got into a car and off I went, down the freeway, right out of Missoula, Montana; and the feeling within me as I departed his sad life resembled the feeling when the train accelerates and the yard sinks safely behind; I am free and for some indefinite period, which while it lasts is as good as forever, my own sad life, with its rules, necessities and railroad bulls, will not be able to catch me.

9.

In Havre, Montana, a long narrow town whose spinal column consisted of a railroad line and a dozen metal grain silos shaped like stubby pencils, trains were memorialized everywhere by such devices as **BOXCARS RESTAURANT AND LOUNGE** beside the overpass to Canada. The railroad yard itself lay just north of Main Street, where Mrs. Gregory, proprietress of the Silver Thimble sewing shop, had once kept her establishment. Hobos sometimes used her outside water-tap, because on the far side of the tracks lay the hobo jungle. She'd tried shutting off that valve, but then they came inside to ask for water, and Mrs. Gregory, who really was a friendly enough sort, turned the tap back on and left them to it. Once a customer rushed in crying that a naked hobo woman was washing herself outside! Mrs. Gregory said to let her be; she wasn't doing any harm.

I never to my knowledge met any of Mrs. Gregory's guests, but

I made repeated acquaintance of the hobo Ira, who clothed in his slimy blue windbreaker and in his smell of old sweat and burning garbage, loped along the side of the road, away from the locomotive off which he'd leaped, first trotting, then running *and running* cross-country from his fear, happy to be asked about himself but afraid to answer, hanging his head, twisting away. He was a pitiable curiosity to me when I first met him nearly a decade ago; now I begin to see that he was my brother. Ask him how life was on the rails these days and he'd quickly insist that he usually took Greyhound. He was toothless, and his weathered, swollen face had darkened until it resembled one of those frozen mummies they'd found in a cave in Greenland. Someone had stolen his false teeth. He said that Nevada was a dangerous place, filled with "lifters," but when I inquired whether someone in Nevada had lifted his false teeth he ducked his head and equivocated, afraid to give up this secret. Where had he been? Well, all over. He was headed for Glacier National Park where there might be a cabin he could sleep in while he, you know, repaired his finances. Once or twice a train had carried him into Canada, but he didn't know exactly where. What were his plans? Well, get a rest, get a little snack, try to improve his finances. All he carried was his bedroll, because he didn't really need to drink water that much (no wonder he resembled a mummy). The worst thing about riding the rails was the danger of falling asleep. Why Ira felt so terrified of failing in his vigilance, whether because of railroad bulls, gangsters or his own nightmares, I never learned. Why had he leaped off that westbound train in Shelby? Because maybe it wouldn't stop in Glacier and it might end up in Seattle; he wasn't sure; he was getting tired; he had to run along the side of the road, hugging his bedroll. Anyway, he didn't really care about that—well, he—he didn't know—anyhow, he had to improve his finances. Had he ever been in Havre? Well, no, maybe, but actually . . . I asked him whether he liked boxcars or grainers better, and in terror he murmured something about hotels and riding Greyhound. His evasions repeated themselves, like his odor of burned cooking and of sooty, dirty concrete underpasses whose ceilings were charred perfectly black; there was one of those to west, in Shelby (they've got a little dugout down at the I-15 overpass, the cop there had told me, and we leave 'em alone if they don't bother our citizens). Can you see those concrete niches between bolted assemblages of metal? That's where the hobos sleep among their bags and groceries, shoes and bottles, amidst graffiti dating back ten years or more: **LEVI T. Louisville, Ky 2-86 Spook-Bound.*** They write their own memorials, or they get drunk or sleep; they quarrel; they anticipate catching the westbound. They lurk there beyond eyesight and windreach, waiting above the steep gravel drop for their dearest train to approach the **NO TRESPASSING** signs on barbed wire below them. But Ira couldn't wait. Give him a ride to Cut Bank, as I did, and ask him how he'd next proceed; he'd reply: Oh, I dunno, just relax, maybe get a little snack, work on my finances . . . —and then on the way out of town you'd see him rapidly proceeding down the roadside, deep in grass, not hitchhiking, the next town miles away. A day later, on the highway west of Glacier, you might run into him again, and he'd be running, never looking back. Pull over, and he'd watch like a dog in equal expectation of a kick or a trifle of scrap-meat. Open the back door, invite him in, and it took him ten minutes to remember you. Ask him any question, and he'd say: Well, no. Well, maybe.

---

*Hobo monikers date back at least to Jack London's time. In his day, perhaps in homage to Venus, they were called "monicas."

I gotta . . . —How many brothers and sisters do you have, Ira? — Oh, I lost count. Anyway, I . . . —He was not much afraid of me anymore; he relaxed and trusted, but could not cease his rapid furtive mumbles, head whirling from side to side. I don't believe that he was dangerous. Mrs. Gregory would have said to let him be.

10.

A lady at the Siesta Motel up across from Boxcars told a more frightening tale about Ira's kind. She said that her brother, who loved animals and never would have done such a thing intentionally, ran over a small dog near the viaduct. The next thing he knew, somebody was knocking at his door. A tall, bearded hobo had come to kill him. The brother was terrified. He found himself compelled to bury the dog in his own back yard, beneath a cross which the hobo commanded him to fabricate. Finally mollified, the dog's master vanished back into the hobo jungle like a troll returning beneath his fairytale bridge.

I use the word "fairytale" advisedly, because mere nasty actuality might have become mythic eeriness in the telling. To be sure, the warning core of that tale contained truth. In sight of the bridge, the parking lot of the Buttrey's supermarket on Main Street, menace walked as a drunk walks, rolling, swooping, obscenely gesturing at the sky. I myself did not feel menaced, and the drunk did no one any harm; he went back inside the Corner Bar and did not even get ejected. But a lady who came out of Buttrey's with a grocery bag in one hand and her child's hand in the other was afraid. It was on account of such stories that Mrs. Gregory, when she considered taking over an empty storefront near Boxcars, which meant near the bridge, was cautioned that her customers, who were mostly women, might fear to park on First Street alone even by day, and so she let that piece of real estate go.

What really lay beneath the viaduct bridge? Mainly gravel and sadness.

11.

And in that narrow strip of mosquitoey trees and grass between the south bank of the river and the old Great Northern Burlington Santa Fe tracks there in Havre, Montana, the wind came through sweet-smelling trees and cooled a **NO TRESPASSING** sign. This had been a hobo stop during the Depression. Where were the hobos now? Dogs barked across the brown-green river. Gnats attacked my throat. Past the **NO TRESPASSING** sign went a bend around which the narrow grassy strip widened into a plain currently rather mucky for camping, plastered with old dogprints and footprints and a few fresh raccoon tracks. Mosquitoes danced golden like evening river-ripples; train-bells sang by. Between the river and the tracks lay a shrunken scrap of forest through which a trail led alongside a barbed wire fence, and though I saw grimy cardboard flats and scraps of plastic hidden under pines and in dandelion thickets, the only shelter I could find, roofed by a plastic tarp weighted down with old tires, held nothing but a farmer's hay bales. There were no hobos in the hobo jungle anymore.

There *is* no hobo jungle, a woman said. They cut down a lot of the trees and widened the road about three years back, to discourage 'em.

An old man in Shelby, Montana, said: Oh, those hobo jungles just kinda dried up. Self-destructed. Alcohol abuse, missing children.

Oh, it's in full swing now, said the officer behind glass at the same town's police station. We see ten or fifteen hobos a week. They're going across the Hi-Line. It always picks up after April.

I'd heard about the Hi-Line from a woman in Townsend who'd sighed: There used to be more of an honor code. You know, honor among thieves. And people used to be more prepared. I was a Hi-Line *winter* rider! I'd get on at thirty below. Never froze, because I carried what I needed. Now people don't ride with gear, and since they don't have any, they want yours.

How often do they get arrested? I asked the officer in Shelby.

We've only arrested one in the last year. Felony assault on a citizen with a knife.

Does the railroad call you in to arrest the train riders?

As long as they keep their feet up on the car or the flatbed, they just let 'em go.

And I saw them going, and I wanted to go, too, like silvery rain blowing off an overpass. I wanted to ride the Hi-Line and get away from this world.

I had one more question for the officer.

He scratched his head. —Do we have a hobo jungle? I dunno.

12.

So were there hobos in the hobo jungle in Havre? The next morning, returning with my sweetheart beneath a sky as steely as the silos of the Farmers Grain Exchange, I set out to explore every inch. We found a camp-hearth with a cooking-pot still on the ashes, as if someone had had to leave suddenly. —It reminds me of Pompeii, she said mournfully. —Passing two kids fishing, we ducked under the bridge and waited by somebody's bedroll for hours. Graffiti proclaimed the self-expression of Gros Ventre Indians, and a camouflage jacket lay in the sand. On the concrete wall it read:

I'm an unhappy hobo
I just have no luck
Even when I ride the train
I ride like old people fuck.

But amidst other grafitti wriggled a pair of SS lightning-bolts beside the ominous letters **FTRA,** which referred to an organization described by Spokane's police detective Bob Grandinetti as *a very dangerous group of people. They are highly mobile and fiercely violent . . . Many FTRA members are basically cold-blooded serial killers who could definitely pose a dangerous threat to police officers.* The same wall memorialized **FTRA KOMO Hopper 97 east-bound 8-21-97 and Freight Train Penny.** How dangerous were Komo and Penny? How might they have compared with Ira, or the drunk in the parking lot of Buttrey's, or the hobo woman who'd washed her only set of clothes behind Mrs. Gregory's store? To the townspeople of Havre, none of whom seemed to have heard of the FTRA, they all might as well have been trolls.

13.

I looked down an alley, and so I saw an alley tramp. The other homeless men I'd seen in Sacramento tended to be busy and unfriendly, but this man took his time, slowly sawing at a packstrap with his razor knife as he sat there among shopping bags, guarding a woman's purse, so I wandered over to him and said: Pardon me, sir, do you know anything about the FTRA?

I know they're a bunch of motherfuckers, he said. I never hopped trains, so other than that I don't know much. But my girlfriend's going to be back in a minute. She knows. She used to hang around them FTRA. She's out getting Chinese food.

A minute went by, and he said: She should be back by now. Bitch.

Another minute went by, and he said: I don't know where we're gonna stay tonight. I got me a hotel voucher, but I been kicked out of every goddamned hotel on Sixteenth Street. (This he said with immense pride.) I used to smoke a lot of crack and bring too many motherfuckers upstairs. I used to punch out a lot of windows. Now them goddamned Hindus wouldn't give me a room to save their lives. They just say: *Sorry. Room full.*

When the girlfriend came back, he said to her: You got any change?

Why? said the woman sullenly.

I gave you five dollars.

The meal was three dollars twenty-four cents, she said.

So you got change. Just checking. He wants to know about FTRA.

Why?

I'm a reporter, I said.

The two of them recoiled, and the man said: I swear I didn't tell him nothin'.

He looked me up and down and said: What are you, some college kid?

Something like that, I said. Are the FTRA around everywhere?

Sure, the woman said. They're just ordinary people. Good folks to hang with if you're catching out.

Why did you used to catch out?

To get from here to there.

I hear they wear bandanas.

Yeah, around their necks. Red or black. The bag-and-tag, they call it. They can be a little bit rough.

That's what I told him, the man said. They got a bad rep.

So how do I meet them?

Just hang out.

And if I see somebody with a red bandana around his neck, can I just go up to him and say, *are you FTRA?*

You goddamned dufus! shouted the man. That's the stupidest fucking thing I ever heard. You wanna commit suicide or what? I'm not even FTRA and you're already starting to piss me off. Don't you get it? We hate you.

Why's that?

Because you're just a goddamned *citizen.*

Sorry about that, I said.

The woman might have pitied me. She said: Why do you really want to meet them? You a cop?

Not me.

They're fine people. Just like anybody else. They only have a different code of ethics.

Like what?

Well, bag-and-tag is the hardest. They get you, everybody gets to beat you up, and then they take a red bandana and everybody pisses on it. Then they stuff it up your face. After that, you're FTRA.*

---

*Years later, my paid acquaintance Pittsburgh Ed, who figures in this book occasionally, remembered about the pissed-on handkerchief, adding: "And you wear it, you never take it off, till it rots off. FTRA, they were pretty good, pretty good. Only problem, man, is they get drunk, they got nobody to fight with, they fight each other. Then I'd say: I've got to get out of here."—I asked him where the FTRA were nowadays, and he replied: "Mostly dead."

Well, I said, now I'd *really* like to meet them.

Go to Roseville. Go to the mission by the tracks and ask for Preacher. He's probably still there sometimes. Tell him Pretty Polly sent you. Oh, I hope I don't get in trouble for this.

I appreciate it.

And stop shaving, the man said. Grow a beard and keep a low profile and stop acting like a goddamned college kid.

There's a camp, Pretty Polly went on slowly. By the rainbow bridge.

If I bring a sixpack, will they be glad to see me?

They'll welcome you then. But don't go into the camp. Just go near and call out, *hey!* Then wait until somebody comes.

And what should I say?

Tell 'em you want somebody to drink with.

14.

I went to the rainbow bridge, and the hobo jungle there was as abandoned as the one in Havre. I went to the mission, and no one told me a thing about Preacher.

15.

You ever run into the FTRA? I asked the hobo in Missoula.

Yeah. I met T. All he is is an overgrown kid with a bad attitude. And I know the Goon Squad. If they know you got five dollars' worth of foodstamps in your backpack, they'll kill you. Goon Squad runs from Portland to Seattle. FTRA goes all the way up through Montana. Wrecking Crew goes everywhere. They're the same.

They're nothing but killers. When I ran into the Goon Squad, I ran into Choo-Choo and Catfish. I bought them Mad Dogs all day long. I got them drunk. Then I had to sleep, and the next thing I knew, they was using my head for a football. I said, I'm comin' back. I got a two-by-four and smashed Catfish on the head. I thought I killed him. I went to the mission and turned myself in and said: I killed someone. But when they went to look, Catfish was gone . . .

Pachacos, they're the worst, he said. They're the enemies of all. It's a family name. They're the big enemies of everybody. I ran into Red. He was on crutches in Spokane. He took off his shirt and on his arm there was a tattoo of a cross and dots underneath it for confirmed kills.

How many dots?

About thirty.

16.

And so they *are* trolls. *Citizens* ought to fear and hate them. As for *citizens,* who might they be, but fearful souls who hate?

17.

Once upon a time the hobo who'd gotten caught in the Mill City ambush in Chicago saw his road brother shot in the back. —I told him, I said, when the first one went through the window, I said, get down. Dummy sat straight up.

And on the trains you gotta watch out for those FTRA gangsters, he warned me, you know, Freight Train Riders of America. All they are is a bunch of punks. They think the railroad belongs to them. In Montana they got a bounty on 'em, because they go around killing people. They used to mark themselves with a big blue or red bandana and a gaucho pin, but the cops finally figured that one out. I knew one guy from them and he turned out to be a real asshole. Liked to get drunk and fight with everybody. I heard he got shanked.

Once upon a time an old man in Helena who used to ride trains all over retired on a piece of gravel in sight and sound of the tracks. He allowed other trainhoppers to camp on his place until they started breaking windows. Bitterly he told me that the FTRA used to stand for Freight Train Riders *Alone.* —Now they rode in bully packs, he said, sometimes up to eighteen of them. They were the reason he didn't catch out anymore.

But a certain Detective Summers informed me there wasn't much of a problem with the FTRA in Placer County, California, because his outfit, the UP, ran a tight ship.

I'll tell you what, said a Burlington Northern spokesman in Fort Worth, Texas. We are aware of their existence and that is primarily due to graffiti we've seen and rumors. But have we had first-person encounters with persons who are members of the FTRA? We don't know. We treat them all the same. Our philosophy is if we find somebody who is riding one of the trains, we treat them like trespassers.

Translation: They're unknown and unknowable. They live under bridges. They're trolls.

18.

I don't know them and they don't know me; to them I'm nothing but a *citizen.* But I've sat in sight of them on my own private patch of double track on a rainy afternoon, and we are all listening like predators to distant engine sounds.

19.

The woman in Townsend who used to ride the Hi-Line (*we treat them like trespassers*) was named Cinders. —Comin' off the train in East Glacier, she'd said, that water's so cold, that spring water, that everybody jumps off the train a minute to taste some.

Cinders was the recently anointed Great Grand Duchess of the Hobos. Frog, the King of the Hobos, had chosen her. She was fifty-five years old when I met her. When she was thirteen she'd run away from home, wandering the streets of New York City, so sad and lost. Then one night in a shelter she met longbearded men with piercing blue eyes who sat around sharpening their machetes, carrying knives and guns and the other tools of their trade. Something happened, she said. They became her brothers. She'd been broken like Humpty Dumpty, and they put her back together again.

She got a reputation for defending herself—that is, for fighting as needed. She said that a rep didn't need to be true. Whatever you'd really done got whispered into strange ears and magnified, like the messages in the party game called "telephone," until you sounded superhuman. That protected you.

She had fine memories. Through open boxcar doors and in hobo camps she'd seen elk at sunrise, eagles. She remembered a boy who'd jumped off the freight to pick her a rose.

Yeah, you think a lot, because you're alone a lot. Even the couples. One's gotta go searchin' the dumpsters for food, while the other has to watch the gear.

Cinders still longed to ride the rails, but she'd grown afraid. She'd broken her back twice, and spinal fusion afflicted her. — There's so many of them big yards now that're hard to get through, she said. Razor-wired like mini-prisons, you know, and dogs chasin' you . . .

(I remembered trying to catch out in Spokane with my friend Scott and spying the double-headlit scooterbuggy with big wheels slowly rolling along on both sides of every single one of those high-tracked, sunset-outlined trains, scooterbuggy on the left and on the right, wriggling and glaring as their hardhatted driver gazed into every open boxcar, shining light into every dark place. Two scooterbuggies, and then a third one came! We got out of that yard. When we tried again, we got cited and warned by a bull who drove twenty steps behind us until we were off the property.)

Heavyset, her red hair going grey, dogged by high blood pressure, attached to her many pets whose needs helped keep her off the rails, Cinders hated *those young guys, those wannabes,* who spray-painted switches black just for the hell of it to cause train accidents, who broke into buildings, who solved arguments with guns instead of punches.

She sighed and said: Not much tramps comin' through here anymore. Used to be kind of a home base. But shelters are not so welcoming anymore, since there are so many homeless, and they have families and I guess it's fair that they come first.

It's just a lifestyle, she said. It's just been abused. Look at those kids killing each other.

That old trailer I just got, she said, I'm gonna fix it up. It's gonna look better with purple flowers painted on it.

Then she said: It's a way of life, a lot of freedom. You can move fast, or you don't have to. You can camp with people, or if you don't like to camp with them you can just leave.

20.

From a certain open boxcar in a freight train heading the wrong way, I have enjoyed pouring rain, then birds and frogs, fresh yellow-green wetnesses of fields. A jackrabbit hopped right past our open door, pursued after the fact by a dog whose modest velocity expresssed resignation to the fact of the fence between pursuer and pursued. And I, chronicler of nature's great doings, have seen it all, at my ease and guarded from rain. The interior of the boxcar was thick with an unknown white powder, probably gypsum or talc, that frosted my pants quite nicely, and at dusk kept the walls cheerily visible for a prolonged interval. After a handful of miles, the train stopped. Steve and I stood pissing out the doorway, twin sovereigns of still mirror-ponds and shiny clean gravel somewhere between Marysville and Wheatland. Later he drank whiskey from my flask and I smoked one of his cigars. When the train began to move again, the rainy darkness had come, and Steve's shadow was a pillar of deeper darkness which marched round and round the walls. Then we stopped again, close by the water-shining headlights and tail-lights of Highway Sixty-Five. We ducked out of sight of a cop car. Then nothing happened. Or, if you like, everything happened; there are any number of hissing and sizzling cars in the rain, and an unknown story inside each one.

In winter, my freight-dreams are very different than in summer. The act of trainhopping in and of itself stimulates the same feelings in me that a schoolboy has in spring when he contemplates summer: an infinite, wild green freedom will soon be within reach! But it is only in summer that that freedom actually grows infinite and green. It is then that I dream myself into the past or even into other universes. In winter, my freedom remains wild, to be sure, but the cold darkness constricts me; I am just as alive as in summer, and thankful to be so, but my body reminds me of its vulnerability. I must not get so wet that I cannot dry off. I must not get too cold. The lone tree with the farmhouse light beneath it no longer invites me into an imaginary possession of the property as it did last summer; instead, it seems like a dismal, even danger-ous spot; I want the train to speed on to the safe warm place I feel drawn to. My boxcar becomes more conveyance than shelter, and instead of thinking about what might be, I interest myself in what is. I remember that on that end-of-the-year night Steve and I talked about our lives and what we had and had not found possi-ble. Although in some ways I hardly knew him, I felt close to him and happy with him. The qualities of a good road companion—considerateness, friendliness, generosity, openness, patience, determination—were such as to make him immediately and deeply a friend. His religion, politics and moral views differed consider-ably from mine. That was, as it always should be, utterly unim-portant. I would gladly have ridden all the way across Canada with him. I trusted him with my backpack; I counted on him to help pull me up into a boxcar when my muscles were aching; I shared my water with him. If he got arrested I would cheerfully have come forward to share his fate.

So we chatted, smoked, drank and rubbed that unknown white dust out of our eyes. I asked Steve how many people he knew who would envy us if they could see us now, and he thought awhile and said: Zero. —That made me even happier.

It was about nine-o'clock, nearly seven hours after we had first climbed in, when we slid off the lip of the boxcar's square mouth and began walking along the tracks into an inexpressibly refreshing night whose frog-songs were as rich in tones, volumes and multitudes as all the recordings of the Mormon Tabernacle. When we reached the head locomotive, we saw that it was dark; the engineer must have gone home long since; our decision to leave this cold dead train was thus proven to be in the same spirit of prudence which is manifested by the lice which leave a corpse. What proud train parasites we were! After an hour we packed away our jackets, drinking in the air with every inch of exposed skin; I especially remember the bliss of cool oxygen, seasoned with ocasional raindrops, on the backs of my hands and on my sweaty throat. It felt wonderful simply to move. My body's happiness became mine. After another hour the horizon grew poisoned by the false dawn of city lights, and the tracks, which had long since gone from double to single, were isolated by flooded ditches on either side. We remembered that somewhere hereabouts was a trestle, and after briefly mistaking a distant headlight for a locomotive-lamp, it occurred to me that this might not be the best place to meet an oncoming train. When a side spur gave us our chance, I prevailed on Steve to forsake the tracks for the road. He did as I wished with his usual good grace, but I could tell that for him, a man who loved what he loved, it was a sorrow to be leaving the rails, and when our asphalt veered away from them, it was almost more than he could bear. Soon enough we had entered the outskirts of Roseville, and could hear the whistles of locomotives and the slamming clanks of assembling and disassembling trains. At eight minutes past midnight we stood beneath the clock at the Amtrak station, gazing into the freight yard. We had already probed our target's perimeter two or three blocks earlier, where in the midst of a grim fence stood a gate with a **NO TRESPASSING** sign, the lock conveniently jimmied for us by our predecesssors. The detritus of a hobo jungle was all under water there, and since the track was single and trains were as absent as any bush or overhang to shelter us from the drizzle for however many hours might be required, we pressed on.

Although Steve, that iron Antaeus, was restored to all his determination the instant that we entered the yard, I had now begun to tire, and the rain commenced falling much harder, so the next three and a half hours grew progressively less pleasant for me. The Roseville yard, which we had been told was the longest in the West,* runs a full six miles from end to end, and we did not know its layout. I had come here twice before, once to photograph hobos and on another occasion in an attempt to catch out with my friend Mike, who when I found us a likely boxcar promptly lost his nerve, after which a policeman escorted us off the property. (On another attempt we made it all the way from Sacramento to Marysville before Mike got sunstroke.) Nowadays it would have been worse if a policeman spied us; for a kindly carman whom Steve and I approached for directions warned that we would be jailed. (Give some people a little power and they turn into Nazis, don't they?) He proudly said that people had no idea how important the Roseville yard was. Why, it was Freight Central for everything west of the Mississippi! If the terrorists ever blew it up, there would be hell to pay. We assured him that we did not wish to blow up any trains in Roseville, and that we would never litter or piss in his boxcars. The carman, young, shaveheaded, a giant, then decided that he liked us. He asked us which way we were going,

---

*It is not. That distinction goes to North Platte.

and we said that northbound would be just great, but any of the other three directions would work about as well. —You ride freights for *fun*! he cried with a smile. He advised us to walk the gravel on the south side of the yard, just off the first track, and keep going until the tracks dead ended, then swing right for the departure yard. It was about a mile, he thought. If he could, he would drive his car over there and try to help us; he called over his partner, who said that a West Colton train would be leaving from Nine Track; so we set out in good hope, water shining gold on cold wet tracks of night; but the ballast gradually grew sharper beneath our shoes, the rain fell harder and harder, the way narrowed, then went toe-deep and heel-deep with water, so we had to clamber over the outermost train and continue westward down our iron-walled alley, which continued at least seven times longer than infinity. Dante says that *midway through the journey of our life* he suddenly became conscious of himself, and realized that he had lost his way. I had decidedly regained my consciousness of myself; I was alive, but only as an aching body that happened to be lost, all right. By a quarter past three we were both longing for a rest, I more so than Steve, and every time we reconnoitered across another train the sweat burst out all over my body because my oil-skin pants, superb though they were at keeping rain and abrasion at bay, hindered me from raising my thighs high enough to get my toe in that first rain-slicked rung; and of course the trains could have begun to move at any time, at which point a slip might be fatal, so I needed to cling and feel my way very carefully, half-blind with the rain on my glasses, and my pack pressed down on me; the real truth was that I was getting old, tired and fat.—All I want is an open box, Steve was saying, any open box. After that they can fucking arrest me; I don't care . . . —He trudged slowly on, and I limped after, feeling every gravel-point in the soles of my shoes, hating the trains around me and the rain on my neck, until finally we got to the end of a train and saw that there was still no sign of any departure yard! Once upon a time near Townsend, Montana, up the slanting green plateau at the base of mountains a long train headed by four dark locomotives rushed by like a string of windblown clouds and I would have given almost anything to be on it; now I didn't care about whether my predestined train went to the mountains; I simply wished for its magic to carry me away from here. We stopped to rest under a dripping tree, and Steve sighed that he could almost sleep here, when just then we saw a long train crawling westward, many of its boxcars gaping most welcomingly. It stopped. We ran for it and jumped into the nearest box! I confess that we should have spiked the door open, but there were no spikes in sight and we were very tired and any minute now this train was going to take us all the way to wherever it was that we were going! I once jumped alone into an open box-car in Imperial County, California, and ten minutes later was riding north; seeing a mirage ahead—the road was sky-blue, deep under imaginary water!—I wanted to go there even though I knew that that sea of sky ahead would flee eternally, just like Ira. And I cannot say for sure that the unknown place where Steve and I were headed was not the same sort of mirage. (If I make this point too often for your taste, I apologize; this book has few points to make.) In any event, our train now began to move, and we exulted. Sighing, Steve lay down and unrolled his sleeping bag. As for me, I squatted down on my pack, and the crotch of my much-loved oilskin pants ripped. Well, maybe it would now be more convenient to pee through. The bright yellow rectangle of light projected through the doorway slowly narrowed and angled backward, dwindling into a single line of twenty-four-carat gold, then dying into darkness. Then there came more lights, too bright and too familiar;—Steve, I said, we're going *backward*. —Oh, shit, he yawned. —We didn't care; we went to sleep. In the morning the rain was still sizzling down, and we were in the middle of the yard. At noon we walked back to the Amtrak station and took a bus home.

Such is trainhopping, with its myriad reversals of fortune and feeling. Because these impress themselves on me so intensely, I never perceive even defeated attempts to catch out as any kind of failure, for one truly *lives more* on these occasions, whose memories, however obscured by night and rain, remain on my mind's tracks as numerous as the trains themselves. This one night alone offered ever so many other experiences, no less precious for being brief: a glimpse of an ancient Pullman car, as fabulous to us as a woolly mammoth, the sudden sweetness of breathing night air after a rest, and, best of all, a spectacular shadow show on our boxcar wall when the adjacent train began to move; every grainer car silhouetted itself in succession, stencil cuts of perfect beauty whose beauty in fact consisted of simplifying reality until even I with my human stupidity became capable of marveling at it—how many grainers had we passed on that night, and how many had *reached* me? What was I missing in my rattleclank journey through life? —Why, almost everything.

Shortly before I set out on that little adventure through Roseville, my father telephoned me, trying to talk me out of it because it was December. That was how it had been when I set off to visit the North Magnetic Pole: he wrote me a long letter which stated that if I went, I would surely freeze to death. Needless to say, I myself dreaded that possibility, and the burden of reassuring him when I wanted reassurance myself brought me near to tears. But all that had been to the good; his apprehensions and mine impelled us to a camping store with a shopping list; my father generously bought me such items as a spare stove, which served me excellently at my destination. —This time there was nothing he could do for me but beg me not to go; once again he was afraid I would freeze to death. I was irritated—I'd come back from the Magnetic Pole, hadn't I?—and sad for him for worrying so irrelevantly, incidentally increasing my own fears—and wasn't that one reason I rode the freights, to cut fear down to size? The latter operation is not unlike brushing one's teeth. It must be done over and over. And here was my father, the man who was always brave, telling me not to be brave. —I still don't understand why you went to Afghanistan, he said to me once. I guess I'll never understand it. —This must be because different kinds of bravery need not understand each other. After all, my father is practical. I am an artistic type; I am frivolous. When I steal a ride on a freight train, I honestly don't care where it goes. What could be more ridiculous than that? Isn't going anywhere the same as going nowhere?— What does one usually see from an open box? —Well, a long flat vista of fences, boggy fields, mountains in the distance . . . —In which case, why not stay in bed for the rest of my life? This would doubtless become its own adventure. After all, life's the Montana bridge under which some hobo has written, with or without irony, **REST HERE.**

I didn't think I could talk you out of it, my father finally said, sadly, and I wish I could have said proudly, because I was just like him. I never tried to explain to him why I ride freight trains. It seemed to me that he would only say: I guess I'll never understand it.

21.

When we were sitting on that boxcar, Steve's cellphone rang. It was his father. —Well, guess where I am? he said.

When he hung up, I asked what his father had thought, and Steve said: Oh, he thought I was crazy.

22.

So what about him, and what about me, and what about bearded Emmanuel who sat in front of the old whitestone Missoula courthouse waiting for the pawn shop to open so that he could trade a women's lavender mountain bike for a sharp knife either folding or lockback because the previous day five Indians had jumped him on the railroad bridge saying that they were going to kill him? Emmanuel said that he said: Well, go ahead and kill me if you can!—and then kicked one of them down. They let him go. On that same day a man accused Emmanuel of theft. Emmanuel offered to let the man search his backpack, and the man failed to find the tiny cassette player which had wound up missing, but Emmanuel remained uneasy enough to crave a weapon. I wonder if the woman who used to own a lavender mountain bike ever caught up with him? And I wonder who Emmanuel's father was, and what he would have made of this journey through life? And I wonder what it means that I am willing to consider Emmanuel my brother, whereas to him I am but a *citizen* to be begged from, avoided or duped? But then I think: Do I truly consider him my brother? Would I leave my backpack with him? Would I trust him to sleep beside me in a boxcar and not go for my throat with his new sharp knife? And if not, could it be that my various books, written in the belief that we are all members of the same human family, are either hypocritical or else as ghostly as boxcars slowly trundling through the northern darkness?

And what about Ira? *Isn't going anywhere the same as going nowhere?* I wrote, but that begs another question: *Isn't running away from everything the same as running toward everything?* In which case, isn't fear the same as happiness? Would I be riding the freight trains if I wasn't trying to escape from something?

How free am I? Don't I skulk like a rat through trainyards? Don't I doze in boxcars with my boots on and without a sleeping bag, so that I can disappear more quickly when emergency strikes? Don't I long for my train to move?

How I love shadow-shows! Particularly beguiling is the way that freeway overpasses fill a rushing boxcar's doorway with silhouetted diagonals. Do I love shadows because I fear the third dimension? Am I a writer and a printmaker in an effort to control my perception of the world by constricting it to my level?

And aren't all these questions, which rush through my mind and depart unanswered, nothing but shadow-shows themselves?

23.

Life spends a perfect moment of itself in Karen's Cafe (Shelby, Montana): What will you *lovely* people have on this *lovely* day? demands the grim waitress. And I think: How awful it would be to live in Shelby. But if I did live there, life would be no more or less fine for me than anywhere. In the meantime, how perfect it is to *pass through* Shelby and then run for the tracks when I hear a train bark in the darkness! I have camped with my sweetheart near Shelby in wind, fire and moon, in rain of sparks and choking smokesmell, lovely rushing wind, the mountains cloud-smudges in the night; in short, I have escaped from Shelby.

24.

I want to escape from Shelby, but I don't want to be Ira or Emmanuel. I wouldn't mind being Cinders. I don't mind being myself.

Where did last summer's zebra-shadows and leaf-dapples on trestle bridges go? That is where I want to go, not forever, just to pass through. Maybe that is what Ira meant when he said: Well, no. Well, maybe. I gotta . . . —And what is there for us to do in life, Ira? What can one do, aside from pass through? —Oh, I dunno, just relax, maybe get a little snack, work on my finances . . .

And we flee in search of last summer or next summer, but there's no harm in it if we know all the time that it's only a shadow show.

I long to ride that long train of locomotives hauling down south to Thermal, then Mecca—look, the Jewel Date Co.! I know that there are no jewels at the Jewel Date Co., not even dates any-more. I suspect that the men in orange blazers who stand on either side of the tracks, watching the faintly twitching spider-shadows of palm trees, would rather be out of the heat—well, wouldn't all of us rather be elsewhere? But only a little bit elsewhere, please, because I gotta . . .

Montana trains crawl high under the rainy sky, heading toward stumpy grey peaks like bearclaws. Whitewater keeps exploding between the moss-bearded firs and spruces, pillowing upon rocks and ledges, then speeding blindly on beneath that gloomy sky. Where does everything go? I want to find out. I want to get to Everyplace, not just Anyplace with its gravelly sidings.

Who can understand me? I ride freight trains in the belief that I can trust myself, that I deserve to be trusted even to be a reckless fool if circumstances so turn out—and, after all, if I am dead as a result of my own folly, I am no worse off than if I died safely and soberly. The most cogent thing to be said against trainhopping is that it is the unauthorized borrowing property of others—corporations, to be sure, not fellow citizens who would be inconvenienced; I am a microbe hitching a ride upon an elephant's trunk! —Besides, so many of my proudest deeds have been unauthorized by somebody that I now subscribe to an aphorism of Lukács's: Breaking a law is approximately as weighty a matter as missing a train.* And when the train throbs and hisses on the track, I'm not going to miss it, not unless some other law begs me for violation! All the same, I am proud to say that I have always followed the advice of an old black hobo I once met in Roseville: *Never steal anything but a ride.*

And because the character of the night ride ahead remains unknown—indeed, it might not happen at all—my life, which like yours is constrained, approaches the verge of vastness; the future will offer me a bouquet of possibilities real and illusory; I'll find true love in a golden land! And so the evening turns as yellow as Union Pacific locomotives in palm-tree light just before the sun goes down— look! Those yellow, yellow machines are tinged with darkening green; at this moment they turn peach color, alive like fruit . . .

---

*Like any pious Marxist, Lukács disdains to feel pleasure, and therefore takes pains to condemn that "infantile disorder" from which I suffer; he even italicizes it: the *romanticism of illegality.*

chapter two

SO QUIET AND SMOOTH AND LOVELY

Not long ago, on a gloriously idle summer day, I lay on my back reading Mark Twain's *Life on the Missis-sippi*. Too much of that book retails the voyage of a man twenty-one years more tired than he ever expected to become. He pretends not to be the paying passenger he is, because once upon a time, in his recollections at least, he lived free, which is to say he was a river pilot. The tired man pads his pages with extracts from other books, including his own. He distracts us with the newspaper statistics of a Progress which in my day has superseded itself by more than a century. *We had a delightful trip in that thoroughly well-ordered steamer,* he enthuses, and I do not care. He praises the *thinking, sagacious, long-headed men* of New Orleans, the *active, intelligent, prosperous, practical-minded nineteenth-century populations* around St. Louis; and I am embarrassed for him. Can these stick-figures on the Mississippi truly be accused of living? But I excuse him: this eminent family man can never again be the river pilot he was, not least on account of those twenty-one years; worse yet, the authority and income of the profession have fallen off, thanks to the superior cheapness of railroad freight. —I wish I could tell him that freight trains are to me what steamboats were to him!

Truth to tell, Mark Twain has lost his Mississippi. Lighted beacons, patented charts and official snag-boats drained off most of the mystery; meanwhile the river itself wriggles ever and always into newness, drowning some towns, stranding others. Rivers, roads and tracks are life itself; in the twentieth century, Kerouac's desperately rapturous self-guided highway pilots will rush from New York to San Francisco, turn round and speed back again; for, as Heraclitus informed us, Cheyenne coming differs utterly from Cheyenne going. No matter; life is merely life. Precisely because it perishes, each moment deserves eternal memorialization. In the first pages, the young ones, Twain describes how his apprenticeship required him to *know* the Mississippi as it then was: to know every point, snag, island and bluff for twelve hundred miles, coming and going, in sunlight, fog, smoke and moonless darkness, to know the depths, reefs and sandbars of the ever-altering river; furthermore, to be unshaken in his mastery of this knowledge. On the Mississippi there is, and I insist always will be, a spot called Hat Island, which no steamboat ought to approach by night. It is dusk now, and the boy's mentor, Mr. Bixby, stands at the wheel. Everyone else is saying: *Too bad, too bad,* and: *We can't make it.* But no stopping-bell rings; the steamer continues downstream! They gather behind the pilot in silence. *Nobody was calm and easy but Mr. Bixby. He would put his wheel down and stand on a spoke, and as the steamer swung into her (to me) utterly invisible marks—for we seemed to be in the midst of a wide and gloomy sea—he would meet and fasten her there.* Scraping over an invisible sandbar at full power, brushing against the island's reaching branches, and escaping them, avoiding a dangerous shipwreck whose position can at this moment be observed only through memory's lens, Mr. Bixby proves the perfection of his knowledge. Towns, years, capes, floods and chapters go by, and Twain reports: *No vestige of Hat Island is left now; every shred of it is washed away. I do not even remember what part of the river it used to be in, except that it was somewhere between St. Louis and Cairo somewhere. It was a bad region—all around and about Hat Island, in early days.* And so Mr. Bixby's knowledge of that place is now useless, and Mark Twain's knowledge of the Mississippi has decayed into forgetfulness in the passing of those twenty-one years. Take this, if you like, as proof that Ecclesiastes was correct and all is vanity. But Mr. Bixby's mastery over his subject was no less glorious for being temporary; furthermore, that the very temporariness of it gives anyone with heart the chance of new adventures! No doubt the Mississippi has been tamed since Mark Twain was a cub river pilot. But it has surely become more wild in other departments. I doubt me not that if I set out to ride twelve hundred American miles on a homemade skiff, without lights or identification papers, I'd encounter many a challenge, and most of *those* in uniform. I have been to the Congo, and I've visited Afghanistan twice. But I would surely need to improve my education if I hoped to outlaw my way from St. Paul to New Orleans without touching bottom.

The face of the water, in time, became a wonderful book. So Twain sums up his apprenticeship, and that wonderful book is wonderfully memorialized in the first quarter of his own. The other three-quarters of *Life on the Mississippi* are threadbare because he strives halfheartedly to engage with a new river to which he remains unsympathetic. The truth is that, forgetting Mr. Bixby's admonitions just as we all forget so much else, Mark Twain lost confidence in his mastery of a place. The mastery remains. The proof of it will be *Adventures of Huckleberry Finn,* which creates a vast, mucky, tragic, wicked, stinking exuberance of life on a remembered Mississppi gilded with nostalgia and inundated with satire. Its pages are equivalent to Huck's days and nights on the raft with Jim: *I reckon I might say they swum by, they slid along so quiet and smooth and lovely.*

Where would I like to slide to? If the rest of my life were summer, and I rode toward everywhere, how would the world open before me? I would be proud if I could sincerely write: *The rails, in time, became a wonderful book.* But that book, if this one recapitulates it, is a volume of romantic solipsism; for I will never trouble to memorize the switchyards between Cheyenne and Phoenix, the most practical routings betwen Fairbanks and Jasper, the signalmen's secrets of the Roseville yard. I would rather just clickety-clack along toward everywhere, taking heed from Heraclitus that since one cannot cross the same river even once, I might as well let my travels be quiet, smooth and lovely.

chapter three

A TAWNY COYOTE LOOKED AT US

1.

Since I had no reason whatsoever to go there, I set out for Cheyenne. When I was young I took a Greyhound bus from Omaha all the way to Oakland, California; and I remember the thrill in my heart when Nebraska's flatness began to rupture into sandy gulleys and outright desert; that commenced the West for me; and then when I looked out the window and saw the train tracks of Cheyenne I felt I'd reached *true* West.

That Greyhound kept going west and west, so that Cheyenne was soon lost. I sat next to a nine-year-old girl from Chicago whose parents were Communists and who was bound for Fresno, which we reached at dawn; when she said goodbye to me I felt sad, missing her immediately and intensely all the way to Oakland. She will soon be forty as I write this. Are her parents still alive? Do they still believe? *She* did. I never thought I would meet an American child who got Mormon-earnest about class struggle, but she surprised me, being Reality herself; and for decades her memory occluded even the recollection of Salt Lake and Wendover at dusk, with sunset doubled upon the Great Salt Lake and all passengers silent within the smoked glass of our darkening bus; nor can I tell you when it was that we stopped in Cheyenne but it must have been in the morning since Cheyenne and Salt Lake are far apart and I saw them both on the same day. I do remember a long still train on the horizon, and prairie grass moving in the wind. The duration of a long past experience out of which a single memory glitters tends to become indefinite: I know that we must have stopped at the terminal, but whether for twenty minutes or several hours I cannot say; and that long train could have been glimpsed for but a moment as we entered or departed the city. Cheyenne changed me at that moment.

Once upon a time I almost married a Cambodian whore, or at least I convinced myself that I was on the verge of wedding her; once I considered moving in with an Eskimo girl; in either case, I would have learned, suffered and joyed ever so intensely in ways that I will never know now. And what if I had gotten off the bus in Cheyenne in the year of my youthful hope 1981? California is only half-western, being California. Cheyenne is one hundred percent western; Cheyenne is Tombstone Hill and lead bullets, gold nuggets and Plains Indians, outlaws and shootouts and scalps, bordellos with off-key pianos and long, long trains — and if Cheyenne is none of these things, so what? I have seen Western movies, so I know what I know. And had I stepped off the bus in Cheyenne, I might have become a cowboy; I could have even been a man. Travelling is a fool's paradise, says Emerson, and I am proud to be a fool; for while the likelihood remains that starting over in Cheyenne would have been no more numinous than an afternoon as in some carwash where drivers lethargically get out of their radio-booming cars, it is our fantasies that impel us, so why not believe in Cheyenne? Once upon a time when I wanted to learn about hobos, Lee at God's Love shelter in Helena, Montana, referred me to Maria, who said: Lee knows more than I do, referring me back to Lee, who said: We don't cooperate on those stories. —As the cliché runs, it's not the destination but the journey that fulfills us, and what a nice journey those two ladies gave me! So to hell with Lee and Maria, not to mention Cheyenne; to heaven with rushing from Lee to Maria and back again, with the yellow-green hills of Montana between Helena and Havre rolling and rolling, staining the highway with yellow dust!

2.

Of course because I had a one-way ticket I was chosen for special treatment; proudly the security man who rubbed his hands all over me announced that any or all of forty factors could have brought about my selection. Gazing into his face with interest, I wondered if he knew how un-American he was. In fact he might not have been human; he could have been one of the sinister fringed pendulums at carwashes, which hideously drape themselves over windshields, giving each car a seaweed cluster's touch. Well, then, I would comport myself like a car without a driver. This was how it felt to be on the road in 2006. He slid his hands up and down my body yet again, and when I turned my head to inspect the dull submission of the other passengers, he ordered me to stare straight ahead. I thanked him for his myriad attentions. Now they were intimidating a fat old lady who could barely walk. Later that year I was seeing my father off at the airport in Spokane, and he got the special treatment, I'd guess because he showed a passport with foreign stamps in it, and as he submissively took off his shoes I felt sad, and then after he had passed through the metal detector the security man made him raise his arms like a criminal, and as he attempted to wave good-bye to me the security man lunged toward his waving hand as if to control it, and, sick and angry, I waved back and quickly walked away.* But soon enough my plane was ascending; and because this summer's heat wave had not ended with the summer, the fields were as yellow as old ledger-sheets, so that Sacramento seemed for once western instead of merely midwestern; and the sight of that buckskin plain made me all the more lustful to reach Cheyenne again. Or, as Kerouac expressed it: *Somewhere along the line I knew there'd be girls, visions, everything; somewhere along the line the pearl would be handed to me.*

It was a rapid, charmless flight to Denver. I forget whether they gave me pretzels or peanuts. Riding by freight would have magnified this distance into the equivalent of a voyage to Madagascar. As it happened, the trains would take me only from Cheyenne to Salt Lake on this occasion. But wasn't that farther than to Europe even so?

In Cheyenne there was a chain hardware store out the back door of my hotel, and also a chain restaurant, and across the highway boxcars were passing into the rain clouds. Two yellow Union Pacific locomotives stopped, hissing and clanking, beneath the **IN GOD WE TRUST, UNITED WE STAND** sign.

I went out for a beer, and when I got back I looked out the window again. Across the long littered plain, which was greyish-brown in the cloudy twilight, that Union Pacific train now com-

---

*Hopefully they saved America by inspecting all the pine cones in his checked baggage.

prised the horizon, and just above it, in the center of the world, the American flag billboard still said:

IN GOD WE
TRUST
UNITED
WE STAND.

I had come to Cheyenne only so that I could travel back to Sacramento, and hopefully get more educated about something. But the longer I gazed at that train-horizon above the swaying grass, the more I realized that I had truly come far, far away.

3.

It was the season of Cheyenne Frontier Days, which is, as some boosters measure it, the biggest rodeo in the United States, and very likely bigger than any on Saturn; in short, the ceremonies should be as lovely as the beer jockey's gold and silver belt buckle. The announcer accordingly began by praying that our sins would be forgiven, and then, after some unknown celebrity had sung the anthem for Old Glory, the announcer cried: You can do louder, Cheyenne! That's *your* flag and *your* soldiers! and everyone clapped louder. The concrete floor was sticky with beer.

Lovely blonde cowgirls with white sombreros and giant boobs were everywhere, and it must have been their presence that invited the announcer's next question: Havin' fun so far, Cheyenne? You gotta *love* this stuff!

Sometimes a cowboy would whirl like a boatman in a whirlpool. Sometimes his riding resembled convulsions under the big lights. It was surprisingly limp, the way they rode the bulls, bob-bing and flopping. They rarely stayed on long.

When a rider fell, the announcer would often demand: What can you do for 'im, Cheyenne? WHAT — CAN—YOU—DO? and peo-ple would applaud, but rarely with great vigor.

Almost all the men in the audience wore cowboy hats. Many had checked shirts, and some had full-on Western finery: tuxedo-like white shirts embroidered with roses, horses or squiggles of night-colored ivy. The blonde possessor of a rhinestone purse rested a hand on her plastic cup and snuggled against another blonde while the loudspeaker played Merle Haggard. The extemely young men with soft cheeks and cowboy hats watched wide-eyed the cowboy from Kilgore, Texas; the moderately young girls cheered with their hands and their mouths for the cowboy from Oklahoma. The many Canadian cowboys got served with a platter of cheerful American toleration. Meanwhile the announcer ad-vised us: What a *phenomenal* bull this is! I'll tell you what!

The stocky, bearded man behind me sometimes worked for Union Pacific. He was an enthusiastic spectator, and it turned out that he himself had once been a bull rider. He said that the experi-ence resembled nothing else on earth. —There's this huge piece of muscle under me, incredibly powerful, and it doesn't want me there.

To me, it sounded not entirely unlike riding a freight train.

I asked him if he possessed any one word to describe his sen-sations on the bull's back, and he replied: Adrenalin.*

---

*About his salvation from being gored by that other sort of bull, the railroad kind, one trainhopper writes: *To escape a brush with danger was rather exquisite afterwards.*

4.

I am happy to report the decided presence of Steve. He and his son had flown in from a fishing trip in Idaho. That night after the bull riding, we drank in a small dark bar with a live country band whose singer, a nearly androgynous hero of cowboy glitter, sang of abandoned homes and lost women until my ears rang. Somebody paid for the last round; I disremember if it was I. Then Steve's son went to another bar, Steve, whom I left with a sensation of guilt, held down the fort at our table, and I walked back to the hotel alone, thinking. A three-eyed Union Pacific locomotive, which in the darkness was almost the color of old blood, slowly eased away from me. Behind it rolled a locomotive painted with American flags. And here was I, an American who hoped to ride an American highball. The train stopped. I spied the driver in the cab, his face and hand mask-white as he gazed across the street at me; perhaps he could even see me. He shut off the engine. A trackman came with a flashlight, illuminating the ground in pitifully tiny wavers.

As I approached the darkness of an underpass not far from the billboard which spelled out **God's Top 10 List,** I felt anxious, as I so often did when it neared time to catch out. I am not a brave man at all, but a cautious, even timid soul who makes himself pull off one stunt after another for his own good. And I entered the lonely darkness thinking: Public space should not be like this; all the world ought to be mine. But how can I make it so? It was certain that if I submitted myself to the hands and orders of security men too often, I would become outright afraid of dark places. Therefore, with my hands in my pockets and my head high, I swaggered on with my best tough face. No one was there. Indeed, it felt less baleful here than in the sudden choking darkness of a freight train tunnel. In a moment I found myself back in the ordinary street night. Pale box-cars kept slamming thunderously against each other in the cool late-ness, the train idling like a rapid robot heart.

The next day some dark cylindrical chemical tanker cars glided by while Old West impersonators loaded up their guns with blanks just as they had done in Kerouac's time, when Cheyenne Frontier Days was still known as Wild West Week (which astonished and disgusted him with its phoniness); after witnessing a few blood-less black powder murders, Steve and I strolled across town to the rodeo ring where a slender young girl stood on a galloping horse, holding the American flag aloft!—O Lord, the announcer prayed for her when she went down with the horse on top of her; she fi-nally got hauled away on a stretcher, covered with a yellow rain-sheet. —Mebbe she'll be all right, said a man behind me. —*The show must go on,* insisted the announcer, and so there came a brave Texan on a bull, whirling and whirling right along with it until it jerked sideways and off he went, into the reddish dirt, which was hoof-pocked and cratered by thrown men.

After the young woman's accident, even though she'd suffered only a minor shoulder injury, my fears crawled back into my chest, so that I understood what my uncle had meant when I was a child and he had remarked that the worst thing about growing old was growing afraid. —His medical record is bigger than the Denver telephone book! cracked the announcer, and, a moment later: I want a big Cheyenne ovation fer a whoppin' seventy-eight points fer *the champion of the world!* That was when I realized how much I admired the bull riders for doing this remarkably pointless and self-destructive thing. Should I admire the bearded man of yester-day any less because he was now too old to ride the bulls? I had always been too old. Indeed, by evening I had come to feel quite apprehensive and miserable, my two fears having to do with jumping on or off the moving train: In my imagination I tried to pull myself up onto the floor of a boxcar and got my chest on but not the rest, and so I slipped under the wheel; or else, leaping off while the train rushed on, I shattered a bone against the railroad ballast; needless to say, this second possibility was much less ominous than the first; no matter what, I would not jump parallel to the train, so the wheels could never get me; all the same, what if I miscalculated? Steve would have attempted to reassure me, but he not only took greater risks in this department than I, he was more physically able to take them. It was his practice to leap almost parallel to the train, so that he could strike the ground running and thereby mitigate some the momentum imparted to him by the train, whereas I insisted on landing almost at perpendiculars to avoid getting caught under the wheels. Arvel Peterson, who hopped his first freight in 1930, advises us to do as Steve does: *You don't swing around like a squirrel, but keep one hand holding on tightly . . . You have to hit the ground running or you could fall and break a leg.* But in *On the Road,* the narrator's half-crazed, innocently tainted road guru, Dean Moriarty, becomes temporarily a brakeman and demonstrates how to get off a moving train: back foot first, then as the train moves away swing the other foot down. So there you have it.

I give a typical jocular hobo story about this matter, told me by a gentleman of experience named Pittsburgh Ed: In a box one time, another guy I befriended, hell, that was over in Tennessee, he said, hell, I'll show you how to get out of a moving boxcar! Had to be goin' about twenty-five miles an hour. He jumped out and took two steps, splattered onto a sign! I don't know if he died or not. Never saw him again.

Walking alone up and down the tracks late that night, I wondered how long I must prove myself. I wanted to let go and become old, which meant, as my friend Ben said, becoming irrelevant. But that sounded sad. So I decided not to get old until my medical record was thicker than the Denver telephone book.

The highway was gloomy at dusk, and the sky chilly and grey, the road shining with ugly car-lights and truck-lights. My original fear had been that we would stop at a siding in the desert and die of dehydration. Now I worried about cold and rain. I felt sorry for myself.

Just past Missile Avenue, down under that highway, I discovered graffiti, a moderately putrid stream, a man's shopping cart and blanket. My colleagues Bulldog and Hopper had left their separate marks; so had Yellow Rose, White Boy, Cold Krast and D.T. Mo announced that he was still rolling. Specifically,

Mo's Still Rollin
27 Sep 01
Roll on Tramps
All you others just
. . . Roll over.

But above this self-assertion was written:

NOT TO RIDE
~~THE~~ THE TRAIN ALOIS

or **ALAIN** or maybe **ALONE**

Someone, I presume Hopper, informed us all:

HOPPER
420 **ALWAYS** 05
A GOOD
TIME
S. BOUND

and Hopper's H owned three horizontals instead of one, so that it stood in for a railroad track.

In that cavelike place, which still another colleague's scrawl officially designated a **HOBO JUNGLE,** a well-wisher expressed determination to **KILL MARY**. It was quite dark now, and it felt sinister to be invading another traveller's camp, whose owner might misconstrue me violently, so I walked back to my hotel wondering why on earth I compelled myself to hop freight trains; the instant I had reentered the lobby, where the android clerk required my identification before lending me the right to insert my plastic key in my plastic door, the question answered itself; and I recovered my loathing and pity. Why is it preferable to me to hunker grimy and thirsty in a boxcar in order to watch this floating world unhindered by glass, instead of sitting clean, comfortable and legal on a passenger train, whose windows are invariably small and dusty? I knew the answer then even if I have forgotten it now; indeed, at this moment I am sitting on a bullet train between Tokyo and Shin-Osaka, rushing toward Everywhere on my laptop with a beer beside me. Never mind that. How long could Plastic America last? How long should it last?* Wasn't a plastic

---

*My provisional answer: Until the end of my life, please! I wish to ride the rails by choice, not by necessity.

what the professional bull riders who exemplifed free-willed
ery caged themselves in every night? They drifted from rodeo
 rodeo; that was somewhat glorious, to be sure, but how self-
reliant could anyone be to sleep in a place like this?

5.

The next morning Steve, his son and I enjoyed our breakfast at the Luxury Diner, where a lovely slender little blonde girl
with dark pencil-thin eyebrows and a sweet smile brought the
food, wearing a Luxury Diner T-shirt with a locomotive on it.
Only Steve's son was young enough to have a shot at sleeping
with her. She moved amidst wall-images of rodeo queens and
princesses as if she were one of them, and the omelettes were plen-
tiful and good. I wondered when our next hot meal would be, and
how its waitress would treat us. Then we said goodbye to the
young man, who was flying home, peered hopefully into the liquor store, which we were sorry to learn would not open for another hour, and approached the tracks, which for our convenience
the railroad had placed a few steps behind the diner. It was late
morning. I was in a mood of excellent cheer.

There are some towns that one must always go through softly, Jack
London wrote. *Such a town was Cheyenne, on the Union Pacific.* This
assertion, made in the 1890s, was founded on the existence of a
certain railroad bull who punched hobos on sight. Cheyenne enjoyed the same reputation forty years later. The bulls were said to
strip-search riders and take half their cash. Nor had they begun to
pull their punches. One young transient saw them club a twelve-
year-old boy until his eye popped out of the socket. Who knew
how hot the yard was in 2006? Not I, and not Steve, either. About

Roseville a wise man had warned London that *the constables are horstile, sloughin' in everybody in sight,* and Roseville was still hot if not necessarily hostile more than a century later, as you see from my photograph of Officer Herrin, who stands on the ballast with his arms out loosely at his sides, grizzled, enigmatic behind his utterly dark sunglasses, with his seven-pointed star-badge, his handcuffs, keys and name plate shining, and behind him there are two tracks and then the Union Pacific train he prevented my friend Mike and me from boarding on that hot summer afternoon in 1997; so London had known what was what; and I kept up my guard concerning Cheyenne. Steve and I strolled onto the tracks, near-twin effigies of middle-aged innocence despite our backpacks, and right away a trackman told us to get out. He did not, however, make any effort to cite us. We asked him how to reach downtown Cheyenne, and he correctly indicated the direction from which we had come. With an expression of well-I-never on Steve's face and imagine-that on my own, we wandered along the shoulder of the yard and reached a highway that ducked beneath the tracks just as in Roseville. Before we knew it, we were back at the underpass at Missile Avenue.

Again I studied over the inscriptions, most of which were as proud as the sign for Missile Drive. Never mind the profundity of **FUCK YOU**; for, as I said, Yellow Rose and D.T. had memorialized their travelling partnership on 9/19/04; moreover, Renegade of the FTRA left us all a pair of S.S. *Siegrunen,* and across a circled announcement, decorated with train-track parentheses and partially obliterated sentiments about the sky and the end of the rainbow, that this spot was an official anarchist **HOBO JUNGLE**,* a

---

*During the Depression, a hobo jungle is said to have existed a mile and a half east of the Cheyenne depot. This could well have been its carcass.

larger hand informed the universe that **RASH HAS SMALL BALLS**. In the daylight the place looked "interesting" rather than sinister. Although Steve, who could not bear to be idle, could muster little patience for such side diversions as this; I pointed out that it was a plausible staging area should we hear a train, and so he was kind enough to abide there with me.

6.

Badger happened to be there, flat on his back on a sodden blanket. He was looking for the woman who'd left him for another man. She'd also stolen his dog. Because Badger knew his rival, he knew that his ex had gone to Montana and so he was setting out on the freights to find her. Was this any better or worse a reason to ride the rails than Steve's or mine? Any time now he would get moving, perhaps even tomorrow. There was a train coming through in the middle of the night, but the trouble was that Badger might not stay awake for it. He thought Steve and me lucky to be partners, because one could listen for trains while the other slept.

He hit us up for booze and cigarettes. The instant that Steve, who always preferred running errands to listening to bums, had departed for the liquor store* to get beers all around, Badger broke out his hip flask and shared whiskey with me; he had plenty of booze and cigarettes already, but it never hurt to get more. When he sighted Steve coming down the slope, he hid his treasures away again.

His tales orbited around alcohol. Twice in ten minutes he told of the time that he got arrested and taken to the cop shop; he'd

---

*Here is another virtue of riding the rails: Wherever you are, you will wait so long that the liquor store will open eventually.

hoarded a fifth of Jim Beam in his pack and the lady cop said she was very sorry to throw it away since that was the very brand she drank herself when she went home to unwind, but rules were rules, at which Badger resignedly concluded: aw shit; but when they let him go, he opened up his pack and the whiskey was still there! This was his great fortune, that for once he hadn't lost something. His story made me very sad.

He said that he had been abandoned beside the railroad tracks when he was five, and he'd been riding the rails ever since. I remarked that in that case he must surely be an expert. —*No one's* an expert on hopping freights, Badger said, swigging his new beer. I know where to get on and where to get off, but I ain't no expert!

Indeed, he once got stuck in Rock Springs for three days. Children brought a gallon of ice cold water to his boxcar every day, until finally the cops arrived and said: *Get out. You're going to jail.* —But the railroad bull overruled them all. He informed Badger that the train was leaving at midnight, and he should throw his gear back on and wait. The bull was right. And, as Badger said: Why on earth *wouldn't* them bulls want me out of there?

In his loose and sturdy clothes, with his Jack Daniel's cap pulled backward, he was quite lordly with his flowing moustache-beard, which could have graced any Biblical patriarch, and although his eyes were small and hard they were not utterly unkindly. What surprised me most when I studied his photograph later was how aged he was; because in person he was sufficiently self-reliant, even commanding, to hide any connotation of feebleness.

Badger advised us to sleep in the whorehouse in Green River. They'd take our identification cards and expect not to see us at dawn.

He told us not to go west on the Union Pacific, but south on the

Burlington Northern. That train wouldn't come until the middle of the night, he said. He repeated that one of us should watch while the other slept. And I supposed that the woman who had left him had been his partner in this way, and again I felt sad for him.

A Union Pacific train was coming. Badger told us not to bother trying to catch out, because no train would stop in the yard for hours. Since no one was an expert on hopping freights, not even Badger, Steve and I ran for it just the same, and it stopped. I called goodbye to Badger, who roused himself just enough to wish us good luck. I will always remember him making the "road sign" of an extended middle finger, lying there on his soaked blanket, all wet.

7.

Our train was pulled by two locomotives. That meant we had merely a reasonable chance of going a reasonable distance. (Jack London again, underscoring Badger: *One never knows, and one must be prepared every moment for anything*) We leaped onto a chemical car with a narrow balcony and hid, after which Steve, superior to me in most railroad ways, went foraging and found another car with a wider balcony, so we decided to take the risk that the train would start and ran down to the better car. Quick, up the ladder! Off with our packs, and lie down low! I felt the accustomed rush of fear. Someone in a hard hat might see us. We lay lower than low, and my heart was in my mouth as I gazed up at the clouds . . . the brakes hissed again . . . and we were departing the yard with increasing speed, grinning like fools.

We passed our hotel. There came a crossing, and Cheyenne reached vainly after us with her last streets. We stayed low. Then there was nothing beside us but grass and highway.

Now that I had time to be more specific in my observations, I perceived that we were riding a hopper car with a wide porch corroded into an eerie likeness of an aerial photo of Arctic ice floes. Perhaps sulfuric acid had been spilled here. I noticed that my naked palms soon began to sting if I left them against the metal very long. Fortunately we both had gloves. Directly ahead, across the coupling, I saw a white thorax with ladders; and at the junction of its V-shaped ribs was a cloaca in which trainhoppers and other trainhoppers could hide. Steve made no bones about crossing back and forth when the train was moving; Jack London would have done it with élan; I would have done it only if I'd had to.

The freeway for Omaha veered left, and then we were out onto the rolling green paririe, with pickup trucks whistling down the other freeway. I felt a pang to be going farther and farther away from the slender girls with silver belts and white cowboy hats and long legs whose presence had decorated Cheyenne Frontier Days. Someday one of them might have married me if I had only tried hard enough. They were now replaced by blackeyed susans and antelopes, then more antelopes behind the fence. Here came a huge refinery, cattails and river willows. The smell of baking creosote, which made Steve nauseous, I always liked; to me it was like booze. Now there were so many antelope on the plains, then lovely cloud-shadows, jade-grey on the grass. The prairie suddenly dropped off on the south side of the track, the horizon as empty as Zen perfection. —Fuckin' *buffalo*! Steve was shouting in ecstasy. Two buffalo out there!

Our lives were as clean as thunderheads. Steve rushed over the coupling, gripped the ladder of the facing car, crouched fiercely and gazed out at the world through his dark sunglasses; he was a king and his crown was a baseball cap; his hands were in brand new black work gloves from a Cheyenne hardware store; he wore a checkered shirt and jeans and threw back his head in regal magnificence.

We stopped in the prairie to let pass another long train with a sulfuric acid car and a hydrochloric acid car, many containers and boxcars all closed, some with graffiti'd faces and initials. A black car of corn sweetener trundled grandly by our corrroded porch. The day was getting hotter and hotter.

8.

Since I am the first observer ever to have travelled in this unknown territory called Wyoming, I ought to descibe the prairie's greennesses, undulations, wildcat oil wells, fences, hawks and antelopes, some of which are black and white. Sometimes one can see the white desert sand beneath the grass. No human has ever been here. Other train riders must gain similar sensations; for after writing these lines in my journal I read the following remarks of a Depression boy, who surely had survival on his mind, but could still feel the joyful wonder of hopping: *Each time we crossed into another state, I felt like the early explorers.*

How can I say what I saw, heard, smelled, tasted and felt in Terra Incognita? You may have visited Wyoming; you have probably seen grass; very likely you've followed a fence; you could be familiar with the outlines of antelopes. But have you seen what I've seen? Did I see what Steve saw? The Tang Dynasty hermit-poet Cold Mountain, who was named after the wild place he inhabited, wrote:

People ask the way to Cold Mountain.
Roads fall short of Cold Mountain.

Ice stays all summer;

fog dims the dawn sun.

How did someone like me get here?

Our minds are different.

Otherwise you could get here, too.

I never could have gotten to Cold Mountain because I lack Cold Mountain's mind. I love cities as much as solitude, prostitutes as much as trees. And I am proud that this is so. Neither the ecstatic openness of Kerouac's road voyagers, nor the dogged cat-and-mouse triumphs of London's freight-jumpers, and certainly not the canny navigations of Twain's riverboat youth define me. I go my own bumbling way, alone or in company, beset by lapses in my bravery, energy and charity, knowing not precisely where to go until I am there. That afternoon I was there, and those Wyoming hours have crystallized within my memory into a jewel of infinite depth, whose contemplation brings me joy.* I possess that rainy night walk with Steve into the Roseville yard, and this thrillingly unbounded Wyoming afternoon, and I believe that I can hold eternity even without understanding it, because all afternoon we rode through green mounds of mystery, with blue table-land ahead, and rainclouds.

People ask the way to Cold Mountain, so where were we? I remember Steve bent over the Wyoming map, trying to place us (a tricky matter, since roadmaps less and less often show train tracks on them, perhaps out of obedience to Homeland Security), and his finger traced a squiggly line and his glasses were off and he

---

*A man who once hopped from Oakland to Kansas City and back seconds my enthusiasm: *Wyoming, I had decided, looked like a fairly crappy state — my judgements being terrain, housing — but Nebraska somehow seemed different, not that it exactly had those golden wheat fields or anything.*

looked old but more soft and kindly than ever, and I felt rich in my affection for him.

By the way, where were we? Well, it was beautiful high empty country, empty in the purest sense. As we passed into the rain clouds it grew cool and the prairie took on the color of jade. My life's anxieties dwindled away by late afternoon. Steve and I lolled on the chemical deck, getting drunk on whiskey and speculating about dinosaur bones and Little Bighorn. I cannot imagine a better way to pass the time.

Through the round hole in the floor, I admired the perfect dark whirling of the wheel upon the silver purity of rail, silver banded with black and gold, the wheel itself blessed with its own rings of whirling patterns.

Presently we saw lightning on the horizon, and it began to rain, and I wondered whether lightning ever struck that long metal caterpillar called a freight train, or, better yet, the tracks it moved on. Very easily I decided what I had about riding the lumber gondola with Steve the previous year, namely, that if I died in this way it would be quick and it would be worth it.* After all, what would I lose if I died on the way? Hadn't I already lived?

A tawny coyote looked at us.

No, I had no reason on earth to go to Cheyenne, not until then, gazing down through the pine meadows into the blue and indigo mountains ahead, wild-hearted beauty that brought tears to my eyes, amazing me that all of this was part of one country, which was *my* country; so that for a moment, in spite of the torturer President we had in those days, I gloried as I used to do in

---

*At the beginning of the twentieth century, one hobo opined that the steel *draws the lightnin'. I saw a bum git struck dead on a track once. It turned him blacker'n a Jew's derby.* But no locomotive engineer seems to worry about it.

being American. Our train ascended past another herd of antelope; they all turned their heads toward us.

Passing suddenly into a tunnel of utter darkness and unknown duration, we breathed through our handkerchiefs, and before our headaches got sickening came out again amidst scattered boulders as we went up into the clouds, and there were more sculpted rocks in the meadow, nibbled away and smoothed like driftwood; I smelled green trees all around as rain pattered on my face and hands. Then through a vaginal cut in the red rock, our freight train pulled us up into the sky, with small pines on either side of the tracks, and the entire world was red like Bryce Canyon or Zion.

It was unspeakably moving. As another ancient Chinese poet wrote:

My way entered Thunder-house, of deep-founded rumblings,
then out into Ghost Gorge, of great precipices.
I gazed on the world's Eight Stays, saw all in the Encircling
Seas . . .

9.

But after hours of these rushings, we rolled back down into the knowable world and found we had gone only half a hundred miles, to the menacing yard of Laramie, where once again we must hunker down against the Union Pacific bulls, praying that we would not stop in their view. Fortunately we rolled on through the yard and the old brickwork city, picking up speed again, with the late afternoon sun in my face and especially on my ears, the etched and rusted squiggles in our car now gilded into filigree, the plains around us yellow and hot, and I remember tall grass and prairies so fiery-gold that my eyeballs ached to look at them, and Indian-looking towns, and I felt very contented cutting Steve and me slices of cowboy jerky with my pocket knife. At dusk we stopped in the smallish mosquito-ridden yard of Rawlins, near the prison. It was here that Jack London once bought his passage on a freight by shoveling coal for a locomotive's fireman, a bit more than a century before.

It was rainy and windy, and we thought we might be compelled to pass the night on that exposed chemical deck, so when another freight with four locomotives pulled in on track one, noble Steve leaped off our train and found us an open box eight cars down, on which we decided to gamble.

As soon as we climbed in, the freight we'd abandoned departed us.

10.

All the same, Steve had scored us a wooden-floored car, good to sleep in, and hardly graffiti'd at all except for someone's initials whose Ш had been fashioned into a pair of nippled breasts. Next morning I would see that a woman's face and shoulders had been faintly drawn around these objects.

Our former train departed rapidly, as I said; so did four others, one of which bore amphibious-looking army vehicles on its flatcars. Steve proposed that we crawl beneath the wheels of one of these, but I argued that that would expose us to wind, rain and bulls. So we enjoyed our customary whiskey and cigars in the boxcar, the cigars provided by Steve; and as we smoked, we sat in the doorway with our legs swinging out, gazing up at the Big Dipper and relishing the warmish windy night whose prairie

wind moaned and whistled almost as loudly as the passing trains.
By then I was done in. Taking off my shoes, I stretched out on the
floorplanks, with the pack for my pillow, and not long after I fell
asleep a whistle screeched in my ear and we were happily off!

11.

Our freight train clanked, stopped and started again.
Then it began to highball toward Everywhere, and its clatterings
became as thrilling as the stamp of a flamenco dancer's feet.

The night grew so cold that I had to break out the canvas paint-
er's tarp I had bought in Laramie and wrap myself in it. We must
have been crossing the Continental Divide. I slept badly, waking
in fear every time we stopped in a yard, hiding from lights and
voices. It kept getting colder and colder.

Dawn was a blinding turquoise slit (this being the doorway,
seen obliquely from the wall). Thoreau advises us to *reawaken, and
keep ourselves awake . . . by an infinite expectation of the dawn, which does
not forsake us in our soundest sleep.* Indeed, this dawn bore more in-
finitude than nearly any I had seen since my childhood and various
solitudes on Arctic islands. It was the blue that this earth might
show to an astronaut: glowing from within, promising, lovely without warmth; above all, far away. The beauty of a welder's flame
possesses some of this character. The eyes of the first girl whom I
ever loved with erotic feelings, the surface of a tropical ocean seen
from below as I ascended from a scuba dive, the agile yet coldly
weighted sparkles within the sapphire ring I thought to buy for the
woman I married, these were cousins of this dawn which was now
offering me grace somewhere in the unknown West.

Presently shape and texture stole back into the world, so that my gaze, led away from me by a lovely trail of light across the woodgrain of the boxcar floor (whose complex beauties can never themselves be improved on), reached the edge of my moving frame of reference and expanded into a newborn desert universe whose coolness had not yet bled away and whose solitudes were unmarred by any spoor of humanity. I stepped into the patch of light, gripped the boxcar door, and gazed out. I have always worshiped deserts, and this one excited me as much as a new lover.

Presently we were in very Utah-like, deserty country, sagebrush golden-brown with long dawn shadows, and railroad cuts in the red dirt. Another longnecked antelope gazed at me as I looked back from the open boxcar.

12.

Steve woke up with a sore throat, but a pull of Jägermeister from his hip flask slowly returned that prince of the iron horse to his enthusiasms. As for me, beef jerky, chocolate, water with lime juice in it and, in Badger's honor, a vitamin tablet washed down with Jack Daniel's seemed the appropriate breakfast for our new country.

The long, immaculately distinct train shadow on the gravel, which was black and white, like kernels of Indian corn, the wonderful silence whenever the train stopped (one of my most reliable souvenirs of a train hop is aching ears), both of these made me wonder whether this might be the place where Fate meant me to disembark and commence my more perfect life; meanwhile, Steve worried because the righthand wall of the boxcar was warm, implying that we must be going north instead of west — and he was right; we'd arrived in Idaho!

In our trainhopper's atlas, purchased in my favorite countercul-ture bookstore in Portland, Steve had located one of the junctions we passed. That was how we knew where we were. From Po-catello we could retrace our journey to Wyoming, God knows with how much difficulty since only He and His engineers know where the freight will stop, or else we could go to Missoula, which was not very near to Sacramento at all. —*Fuck!* Steve shouted.

Meanwhile, winding gently upward between the sagebrush hills, we went wherever we were meant to go; and I tried to nap while Steve, guarded from the world in his jacket, cap and sun-glasses, gazed out the boxcar door at the haybales, a watchful, wistful silhouette of an astronaut in an unknown world.

13.

Once upon a time a young man named Ukla wrote in his journal: . . . *this whole trip was fucken nuts, its just the way the world looked with the lightning flashing spectacularly in the dark night, watch-ing it all roll by as I layed back stoned in a most peaceful haze feeling completely at ease and in awe of everything around, one of the most beau-tiful moments I've ever witnessed.* The next page of the same entry records his astonishment about going *from such a state of intense beauty watching the lightning storm to being layed up by an aching side with winds howling down my back and my clothes flying around in some field behind us* . . . because, as trainhoppers learn very well, things change.

We were both sleep deprived and dehydrated. I possessed about three-quarters of a liter left out of my three liters of water, having been on the road only twenty-five hours.

Our train stopped. This time it really stopped.

By midday the air in the boxcar was quite hot and dry, so that I began to confuse the sound of the grass in the breeze outside with the nonexistent sound of the train pressurizing preparatory to moving.

I wanted to lie down and sleep as Steve was doing.

Each scratch and chip of the boxcar's white paint had now assumed its own shape: I still remember the parentheses, the lizard, the charcoal impression of a nude woman from torso to knees, the minuscule silhouetted side view of a high heel, the parallel diagonal lines. And each time I heard the whistle of an approaching train, I *hoped*. The train blared by, its steel vertebrae clanking individually, some of them tagged with such admonitions as **DESTROY THIS TRAIN**, others marked with nearly illegible initials; and then the last car shot by at immense speed; and again I saw the sagebrush, the barbed wire fence, the highway; and I waited for the hiss of pressurization which did not come. The interior of the boxcar grew hotter and hotter, and Steve lay sluggish and gloomy, and my water was nearly gone. Was it better to bail out of this hundred-degree heat and hitchhike or walk to the nearest town, in order to get water and somehow pass to the next railroad line? Or should we sit tight? Pocatello was only sixty miles away — too bad that we'd never wished to go there . . .

14.

I could see what appeared to be a highway maintenance station on the far side of the highway. In most of our previous stops since dawn there had been no highway, nothing. I proposed to Steve that we seek water there if our train did not start in the next hour; he consented, and the hour passed.

Once we had leapt out, descended from the ballast, waded through the tall grass, worked our way through the barbed wire and crossed the highway, I looked back to learn how long our train was, and it was truly long; it went on and on like the tree-seasoned desert mountains behind it, and on one boxcar a painted face gazed at me. Steve was too hot and crabby to notice.

15.

We walked five miles to Soda Springs. Steve continued to be less than happy. As for me, I wondered whether Badger had been an expert after all, and we should have caught the southbound BN train out of Cheyenne. How luxurious speculation is! That five miles took more than long enough for me to consider every possibility.

In 1938 a girl named Phoebe Eaton Dehart, who had caught out of Cokeville, Wyoming, with her friend Irene, arrived in Soda Springs. *We shared a pot of beans with a couple of cowboys who let us sleep in their tent.* They went to the rodeo, and the next night Irene got involved with one of the cowboys. But when Steve and I explained that we had come in on a freight, we excited surprise and doubt, because nobody knew of anyone doing that around here.

We dropped in at the country club for a beer and they were nice to us. Then we got separate hotel rooms because Steve said I snored more loudly than the boxcar itself.

Next morning after a giant breakfast the barmaid and her friend the cook stood for my camera under the bingo board at Mom and Dad's, with cowboys on horseback on the dim wall behind them and a titanic bottlecap resting on a rack of horns.

16.

After some negotiations, Steve waiting outside (for on our expeditions he is the traincar-finder and I the people-pleaser), the hotel clerk found a certain Judd to drive us south to Ogden, where hope and our trainhopper's atlas alike gave us a straight shot to Sacramento.

Judd believed in freedom, hated the Democrats and Republicans equally, and thought it was politics that had prevented us thus far from kicking ass in Iraq. His son was stationed over there, drilling Iraqi Guardsmen. That boy said that we'd be in Iran before Christmas.

Judd hated the Department of Fish and Game; he hated what the government had done at Waco and Ruby Ridge; he loved the mountain towns where nobody told you what to do. His principles were as bright as the brilliant silver metal of the bleachers at Cheyenne Frontier Days.

We rushed southward down the highway, exchanged Idaho for Utah, and reached Ogden's multitudinous exits. None of us knew were the trainyard was, so I suggested that we try the city center, and almost right away we saw track rushing east and west! Then it was the merest matter of turning in the direction of the oldest buildings, and there lay our steel spiderweb . . .

17.

As for us, we had no wish to be flies; indeed, the Ogden yard was very busy and menacing (one old time hobo assures that *I never had anything but trouble at Ogden*); fortunately a long train curled westbound, and a construction truck sat waiting for it to pass, which meant that our ride must be leaving imminently. Paying Judd and shaking his hand in a rush, Steve and I scuttled across the unwelcome open brightness of the rails, knowing that although doing so exposed us to the control tower, the sooner we departed the yard the safer we would be; and so we found ourselves clambering up the ladder of another chemical car, this one with a cramped deck and not much of a roof, there being nothing else available. Hunkering down in the gypsum dust, we had not many instants to duck our heads down before we were off; it was eleven-thirty in the morning and ninety degrees. I felt the old exultation and relief; not only had we escaped Ogden, we were clicketyclack-etying to Cold Mountain!

18.

So far the line went parallel to Highway Fifteen, so we were treated to poplars and grass on Gentile Street, where a man was mowing his lawn. We started and stopped in various small yards or substations of triple track, our hearts leaping with fear at every construction crew or white vehicle. Here was the irony: in the interest of becoming freer we simply gave ourselves cause to dread every last soul in a hard hat... Moreover, it was getting hotter, and we began to wonder if we were going the wrong way again, south instead of west. Reno and Ogden connected by rail in Jack London's time, so they probably still did; of course, unlike us, London had lived the life; he had known what he was doing.

I discovered that tonic water tasted disgusting when it was spit-warm and flat. To express this important subject more precisely, I learned that the hotter a liquid gets, the sweeter it tastes. I forced myself to keep drinking it down; for the day was now remarkably hot, the shade of the diagonal rib indifferent, and soon heat was coming dizzyingly off the metal.

Another train came by, close enough to touch. Steve was in concealment on the other side of the deck . . .

An hour had gone by, and we were scarcely out of Ogden. Our junk train continued to stop frequently and for long intervals. I've since learned from Pittsburgh Ed that it could have been worse: We could have found ourselves on the infamous Modoc Line. —Never caught the Modoc, reported that gentleman, whose longest consecutive stretch on a train endured twenty-three hours. —It's a drag that goes from Ogden to Missoula, he said. It stops everywhere. I've heard people talk about it. Something like thirty-six hours, forty . . . —And we were now less than three hours out of Ogden. At one such halt, alongside the freeway, I gazed for more moments than pleased me at a white shoulder with a pale green meadow attended by cottonwoods. I wondered whether Steve and I would have the pleasure of sleeping behind those trees. The brakes hissed; we finally begin to move again, pausing soon after in a double track with a steeple-less Mormon church on either side of us.

I tried to persuade myself that this was what I had come for, to see and be scorched by what I had seen; and it was true that grief did not infect me as it did in airports, malls and that plastic-carded hotel in Cheyenne; I felt that the Utah around me, while often ugly, remained *real*. If this was not what I wanted, then what did I want? I might have asked to go *faster*; but in that case why not give myself once again to the efficient invasions of security men? I felt no need to be home; otherwise I never would have left in the first place. So what did I seek? In an instant and for an instant I found it, when between refineries, on a small street of green lawns, and just over the Union Pacific fence from me, a blond boy and a blonde girl in bathing suits were just about to step into their wading pool, and then hot chemical winds massaged my face, and we came to a stretch of old houses, warehouses and brown grass as the train finally began to go faster, coming now into brown fields and dust-silvered cottonwoods.

19.

Had I lived my life out on that street of green lawns, or even had I come from far away to visit the house where those children lived, the sight of them in the pool would have meant nothing to me beyond whatever personal associations I would have formed by them; as it was, because I was hot and thirsty and they were in the blue water, because I had become momentarily aware that I knew neither where I was nor where I was going, because even if I could have located myself in some meaningful way it was unlikely that I would ever come back here, much less meet these children again, not to mention learn so much as their names; because what I had seen of them was chance and I could not control even the duration of the seeing, and because in consequence of a different chance that boy resembled the child I had been, and although the girl did not bear much similarity to the sister I had had and lost, she was nonetheless his sister and of about his age (I cannot remember whether she was older or younger), I was touched by a golden pathos almost entirely purified of sadness, so that in those children I did not even consciously see myself; they took on for that instant a perfect life of happiness and coolness whose sentimental fictiveness could not undermine it; because they were truly about to be cool in that shallow plastic pool, you see, and they held hands, while my throat was dry, my forehead ached with thirst and I was going away. In fact, I was gone. Steve never saw them.

20.

To rephrase the foregoing, when you gamble on a freight train, it is so much like life; you don't know the future. (Badger again: *I know where to get on and where to get off, but I ain't no expert!*) You want so much to go to, say, California, and it seems reasonable that you will get there; but your reasonableness may not resemble the train's.

We should have taken the Southern Pacific across the Great Salt Lake. Well, well. And so by the time our freight stopped (I all the time hoping with sick anxiety that it would not deposit us either in the yard of a poison-clouded refinery or in the bleakly exposed multiple tracks of the main yard), we had gone a magnificent thirty miles from Ogden to Salt Lake, which Eddy Joe Cotton's hobo mentor Alabama characterized for him as *a shit hole. Infested with half-minded homeless people and old tramps that got lazy.*

21.

We arrived on the most inconspicuous track, the last one, right next to the road, and when we slipped off that side of our freight car, it is very possible that no one saw us leave, and whoever might have seen would almost certainly not have cared.

A botttle of patriotically cheap and watery American beer lay empty in the gravel beside the concrete slab where the beer drinker had very likely sat, and then past the upended sign a power pole rose on the left and two metal assemblages on the right crowned by sunflower-disks; in the middle ran the track, whose parallels almost touched by the time it went beneath the overpass which cut into one of Utah's desert mountains. We grew astonishingly familiar with this slab over time, and also with several other equally scenic places.

This time Steve was tougher in the heat than I. I kept feeling dizzy and wanted to drink more of my blood-hot tonic water. Neither of us was happy.

We walked much of the length of the yard, ascended a highway overpass to observe the tracks like the conscientious insurgents we were, noticed that our train had not moved and evinced no disposition to do so, in which case it might indeed be called a junk train, and after these proceedings we needed to sit down by the road and wipe our faces.

The day before yesterday there had been cows silhouetted on the pale jade prairies whose infinities seemed effortless from the deck of that chemical car in Wyoming; I'd drunk whiskey at my ease while the world rolled perfectly by! Life had been as inviting as tracks leading everywhere, shining within the frame of the boxcar's darkness I lived in. Yes, I live in a frame! How can I enter the picture itself? But as soon as I do, or not long after, it loses its magic, which is why I want to travel again. Was the magic ever there? Was I or "reality" to blame for its destruction?

22.

Searching for a place to lurk until our train to Everywhere arrived, we crossed another overpass and met Sheldon. Most of all I remember the grass and burrs all over his dark and stinking shirt. I remember that half of his snaggly teeth were missing, I remember that one eye was open wider than the other, and I recollect very well the two pale lumps on his left eyebrow, but his smile was so gentle and loving and good, and he was so shyly patient the way he stood there with branches poking into his wrinkled neck; he was as lonely and eager to play as an abandoned child. He cocked his head at me and asked me again and again if I might be going to Los Angeles.

I told him that we wanted to go west, and he said that it was much better to catch out of Ogden than Salt Lake. I told him that we had caught out of Ogden just now and did not want to go back, but Sheldon merely smiled and expressed the hope that we might be going to Los Angeles.

Steve could scarcely understand him and had little patience for him, so he continued on in the heat, trying to find the best way back to the tracks. He came to a dead end.

Sheldon seemed to possess little more memory than an invertebrate; it was his lonely hope, ever so often expressed, that we might be travelling to Los Angeles, in which case we could keep him company, that exasperated Steve most of all; of me he remembered neither my name nor my destination; and yet his smile was sweet, and when I asked him, he knew the way out quite well, a secret way through a hole in the fence which could not be seen even five feet away, so that Steve, gloomily and skeptically following me, was amazed that I had somehow discovered the invisible road down the steep grass to the seemingly impassable concrete wall and from there through the cunningly broken wire and then down five feet to the street. For Steve was usually the one who led us.

Sheldon smiled at me. Had he been a woman, I might have loved him. If I were a better Christian, I could have considered the possibility that he was the One. He worried that Steve would be injured, because when he had reached that same dead end not many days or weeks since, a car had struck him, fracturing his shoulder. When I looked back at him, this lonely, maimed, affectionate soul was waving at me, gently smiling.

23.

In contradistinction to the gentle, helpful waitress at the Luxury Diner in Cheyenne, the waitress at the Mexican restaurant was disgusted by us, and when we asked for a table to sit at and a glass of water to drink while they were making our prepaid take-out order, she told us to wait outside. To us she became at once a *citizen,* hence our enemy. I am quite aware, although I refuse to believe, that at this juncture the Luxury Diner waitress would have likewise invited us into the great outdoors; we stank. At any rate, I treasure my grudge against the waitress at the Mexican restaurant, and comprehend why it was that in Nebraska, where the young trainhopper named Ukla and his two comrades received no heroes' welcome during their long ride of 1973, Ukla decided that *the men look like Elmers and the women like Louises, stereotypical mid-west folk, kids got the short-shaved in front, long tails in back haircut, just don't understand how these people could be so far behind . . .* And once upon a time in 2006, on a hot Portland Sunday morning on Southwest Eleventh, a wiry man lay on the sidewalk with his head on his pack, and a woman sat beside him, wearing, as street people so often do, surplus army greens; so I asked if either had caught out and the man shook his head with the least possible amount of effort, while the woman said: I have. What about it? I offered her five dollars for a story, and she said: Not right now. —Suits me, I said.—I saw that couple again on the way to dinner, and the woman tried to sell me a collar, a *cute* little collar, she called it, because they were *hungry.* I repeated that I wanted to buy freight train stories, and she said she wasn't in the mood because all her freight train stories were sad. At this point the man, deciding that he must have caught out after all, weakly offered to tell me a story about crossing the desert on a freight train, but the woman cut him off, demanding with increasing rage that I buy something so that they could eat, and when I said that I would look them up on the way back from dinner to see whether she felt like selling me any freight train stories she sneered: Isn't that nice? You make a point of telling us that you're going to eat when we're hungry! I don't have time to tell you any freight train stories, you *sonofabitch!*—I felt momentarily hurt, angry and revolted; but who was I to know how the sadness of those freight train stories affected her, and what part *citizens* had played in them?

As for Steve and me, I suppose that to that waitress at the Mexican restaurant in Salt Lake, we were equivalent to Sheldon in his tick-infested grass, poorly hidden in the trees beside the freeway; doubtless *citizens* feared him.

Not caring to stand in the heat any longer than we had to, we kept asking for a table until we found somebody who gave us a more congenial answer. Then we sat down, but they never brought us water.

24.

I was sitting on a loading dock with Steve, drinking beer, eating the Mexican food, which he had paid for because it was my birthday dinner, and we were avidly spying on the trainyard.

The engine driver clambered up into his corn-yellow unit, rang the bell and immediately started rolling, half hidden by a closer train of container cars; and slowly, hissing, smoking and tolling, the four locomotives pulled out, followed by their slaves, gliding through the underpass.

That was the train we had come in on. Did we err, to let it go now? It had been so slow and ineffective, but perhaps now it was highballing all the way to Cold Mountain, which would have been Sacramento until we arrived home. At any rate, we let it go.

After a century, a tattooed man drove up to our loading dock and gave us each a bottle of cold water. I felt very blessed then by the deliciousness of his kindness. He asked what we were up to. I told him. He was a contractor who picked up engineers and drivers whenever he was told. He advised us that only the far track went westbound; all the others went north. He also said that since a child molester had recently been caught (the little girl was dead), Salt Lake was particularly unfriendly to transients, and we needed to avoid the bulls more than ever.

After that, we were sitting under a mulberry tree in the corner of the beer factory, a few steps from the tracks. Steve picked me two mulberries. We set beers in our bag of melting ice, poster boys for public intoxication with our bare feet on the sidewalk. It was cooling off rapidly, the coolness coming first from the grass we lay on; suddenly the evening was very pleasant. It had been a hundred and four degrees; soon it would be ninety-five. The smell of vegetation freshened and strengthened with the approach of night. Meanwhile, the dark-tipped many-windowed dome of the state capitol dodged in and out of container cars all speeding in the wrong direction; and every now and then the *citizens* across the street would go visiting; they avoided looking over at us.

25.

At ten that night I was sitting with Steve against a building, each of us on a throne of two old tires and a single cricket was singing. At first I thought us as lordly in invisibility as we had been in the poison oak of San Luis Obispo, for we were situated in the shadow against the wall, cars coming rapidly around the curved road, their headlights dazzling; but then I noticed that when the lights found Steve, who was more exposed than I, the drivers would turn their heads upon us both; every now and then some generous motorist would bestow on us an obscene gesture. We were roadside trash. But for that very reason we remained nearly as free as if we had been unseen. Of course it lay within the power of any random sadist to do us harm, but there was no convenient stopping place on that bend; and, besides, doing evil takes more effort than speeding contemptuously on; no doubt the balance of them did not even feel contempt, but dull surprise at most, and that forgotten before the next bend. Until it grew so late, or early, that Steve referred to the time as *zero dark thirty,* one carpet-cleaning truck did keep passing slowly back and forth, picking us out with his headlights while we squinted downward; but I suppose that he has put us out of his memory by now. Our invisibility consisted of this: We were just two filthy men sitting in weeds and darkness. And so we told over to one another the highlights of our immense adventures and explorations, all the while listening for train whistles as our gazes idled past the bushes into the clouds and all the way up to the pale freeway overpass on which we'd recently walked to meet Sheldon, who might or might not have been broken almost to incapacity; and I wondered whether he would ever reach Los Angeles; and I also wondered whether Badger had yet caught out in search of his Diesel Venus in Montana. And so Steve and I sat solving all the world's problems, as my grandfather would have said; and then we tired of conversation, for it was very still and humid; and I squashed a tick that had bitten my thigh while Steve sang his own version of the scarecrow's song in "The Wizard of Oz": *If I only had a train . . .* —At our left the railroad gravel was pale and then, very black, the long smooth rails went everywhere.

26.

We never caught out of Salt Lake. Finally we flew home. The instant I got back to Sacramento, I shouted to myself: *I've got to get out of here.*

I THINK WE'RE IN SWITZERLAND, CAT

1.

Where do the freight trains *really* go? —To the Big Rock Candy Mountain, I suppose. Wherever that is, it must be somewhere in America.* I lack the right-mindedness to find the way to Cold Mountain, but this other place beyond the imagination of Chinese sages is mine. Never mind that I'm not yet there; nor that I feel sad to heartsickness, nor that I was not the first to Americanize and even Californiaize Cold Mountain: After the final train hop in this book I finally began to read a present from my friend Paul, the reissue of Kerouac's *The Dharma Bums,* and found it dedicated to a certain Han Shan. Turning to page one, I read: *Hopping a freight out of Los Angeles at high noon* . . . By page fourteen, Kerouac was already going into raptures about Han Shan, who happened to dwell and

---

*One evening, when the great conservationist and nature writer John Muir was still a boy in Scotland, his father said: "Bairns, you needna learn your lessons the nicht, for we're gan to America the morn!" and Muir immediately visualized "boundless woods full of mysterious good things; trees full of sugar . . . millions of birds' nests, and no gamekeepers to stop us in all the wild, happy land."

write poems in a wall-less house called Cold Mountain. By page twenty-five he was off for Mount Matterhorn. Well, I've been there, too. —I sit alone in a faraway airport, waiting for the hour when the baggage of my life will be accepted so that I can approach the metal detector and get my American-ness inspected. Sometimes I am low enough to wish that the security man accepted me, waving me without question into what the regulations now refer to as the "sterile area"; that could be the case only if I carried with me nothing extraordinary. But I watch my fellow passengers stroll down the gleaming floor, pulling their lives behind them in humming-wheeled suitcases, carefree about exposing and submitting themselves, and I envy them because submission is grace. For his part, Cold Mountain's eponymous and decidedly unsubmissive sage goes home as gracefully as the railroad man in the Spokane yard who swings one foot up onto the lowest rung of Union Pacific Locomotive No. 1308, grabs on and rides away with the train, while I stand in gravel watching. And now as I lie in the gravel with my head propped against my backpack, watching the clouds and drinking down a can of beer, a wild California nightscape slides through my mind, bookended by towers of lumber; I'm riding my thoughts toward Santa Barbara, and en route I'll have a shot at Paradise. I may be alone, but like Cold Mountain I am not lonely. *Hoboing is a lonely business* . . . remembers Mr. René Champion, who practiced that activity during his Depression youth. *The wide open spaces of the West enhance the feeling of loneliness* . . . But *what kept me going was the freedom of it* . . . and now that he is an old man, the sight of a freight train brings him near to tears because *it is such a sharp contrast to the life I live now, which is completely organized* . . . Slowly he approaches the security man, wheeling his freedom behind him.

Guitar Whitey, who first caught out in 1934, when he was thirteen, returned to the rails in 1972. He was still doing it in the 1990s, and for all I know he is still doing it now. Naturally he said, as people always do (and they are always right), that it was not the same. Nowadays an old bum with a backpack who knocks on doors asking for food will get the police called on him fast.* Moreover, *the railroads have everything zipped up so that there is hardly any place to ride anymore. Used to be you could get into a boxcar and there might be ten or twenty guys waiting to give you a hand up.* Nowadays if anyone was in there he would be afraid of you. Meanwhile the glaciers are melting and the sun is getting older. All the same, there went Guitar Whitey, known to the security man as Robert Symmonds, Depression survivor and successful retiree, clinky-clanking off to Everywhere for the sole reason that he wanted to.

(Where is Everywhere? Ask our greatest praiser of freight trains, Thomas Wolfe, and he will advise you of the *huge gaping emptiness and joy* as the freight cars *curved in among raw piney land upon a rusty track, waiting for great destinies in the old red light of evening upon the lonely, savage, and indifferent earth.*)

Every time I surrender, even necessarily, to authority which disregardingly or contemptuously violates me, so I violate myself. Every time I break an unnecessary law, doing so for my own joy and to the detriment of no other human being, so I regain myself, and become strong in the parts of me that the security man can

---

*One journalist of my own time concludes that homeless sweeps have become *far more vicious than during the Great Depression* because their victims no longer have even occasional economic value. In the old days they could have joined the labor force for a spell as fruit tramps. For my part, I suspect that as the attitude of *citizens* toward them has hardened, the character of migrants has altered accordingly. The hobos of London's time were more self-reliant and perhaps more violently criminal than the unemployed men of the Depression, who in turn lost both hope of a job and the skill to do it as they metamorphosed into the Iras, Badgers and Sheldons of my time.

never see. My favorite moment in *On the Road* is when the narrator and his road friends, having arrived in what is for them almost the farthest possible place from their origins,* namely, a lovely whorehouse south of the border, ask for mambo music and are *shattered . . . in the realization that we had never dared to play music as loud as we wanted, and this was how loud we wanted.* (William Blake: *The road of excess leads to the palace of wisdom.*) When I ride the rails, I don't wish to go just anywhere; I demand to go Everywhere. I insist on being myself more than would please the neighbors. So I hereby say goodbye to my neighbors. Turning my back on *citizens* like me, I raise my scratched mirror of a hip flask to the long bend of a freight train seen from an overpass in San Luis Obispo, the unlikely beauty of freight cars, tracks and fences all bending in parallel toward the California mountains.

Not long before 1924, a rather brutal† literary hobo named Jim Tully once stole a Bible from a preacher and used it, assisted by a pack of lies, to get money from the credulous cop who arrested him. The cop's wife blubbered all over him. Then Tully hit the streets and made fun of his victims, who after all were mere *citizens.* (I still remember the lordly contempt of the hobo in Missoula who for five dollars pulled his hat down over his eyes, crossed his legs and gazed into my camera lens, sitting in the grass beside the freeway.) I am not averse to making fun of security men, but I would never be so low as to jeer behind the backs of my benefactors. Well, perhaps that's merely a matter of style. Tully explained

---

*The farthest place of all is Mexico's capital, *the great and final wild uninhibited Fellahin-childlike city that we knew we would find at the end of the road.*

†I make this judgment based on his autobiography. Since making it, I came across these words in another hobo's reminiscences: *Even at this late date I will affirm that I and fifty thousand other bos would have welcomed the chance to kill Mr. Tully,* evidently for pedophilia.

himself almost as Cold Mountain would, assuming that Cold Mountain would ever have troubled himself to explain: *The imaginative young vagabond quickly loses the social instincts that help to make life bearable for other men. Always he hears voices calling in the night from far-away places where blue waters lap strange shores.*

Only Cold Mountain can reach Cold Mountain, and Jim Tully's strange shores will never be mine. In 1991 the young man who called himself Eddy Joe Cotton hopped his first freight train somewhere in Wyoming, evidently because *I wanted to get to Mexico. That was it.* His father had given him a Mexican postcard with a señorita on it. As for Guitar Whitey's *that was it,* only Guitar Whitey knows.

What about Bill, the clean, softspoken, slender greyhaired Vietnam veteran who had ridden the rails across America? When I asked whether he had seen beautiful things, he smiled secretly and said: Of course. I'm a country boy — which I take to mean that he beheld wild or at least rural beautiful things. On one extremely cold occasion an eagle flew into his boxcar and gazed at him as if to say, I'm cold, too, and Bill fed the eagle some of his hamburger and it stayed with him for many hours. I could tell that that memory brought him joy. The rest he kept secret.

Ah, the Smokies! cried half-a-million-miler* Pittsburgh Ed when I asked him what had been his most beautiful thing. The big lake with steam on it that looks like steam, that's why they call it the Smokies. And no highways! Beautiful! Got there because I caught a wrong train. We didn't know which way it was going. Went out of New Orleans... — I asked him if he had been tempted to get off and start a new life, and he replied that he had

---

*"I got half a million miles under my butt. Used to be called the train rider from hell."

not, because another train might never stop there. — Besides, he said, it might not look good in the dark. All kinds of critters out there.

A friend of a friend got *ambushed with rocks* and had to jump off at twenty-five miles an hour to avoid the police. All the same, he cherished his trainhopping times, because the train rocked him so wonderfully to sleep and because *of course I saw things I would never have seen otherwise.* In other words, he reached Everywhere.

Remembering the man who'd trainhopped from Oakland to Kansas City back in 1993, I called him up and inquired whether he had reached Everywhere, and he replied: Did we get where we were going? I guess so. The experience was pretty profound and exciting. —His Cold Mountain, like Bill's, remains semi-private. When we were sitting on the riverbank together in Portland and I asked him what his most beautiful place had been, he finished his beer and said: Well, of course, most of this is off the beaten path. I've taken the U.P. back from K.C. to Portland, and I came along the gorge. Then the ride from Reno back to Roseville, I recall that was just magnificent. And the ride through Moss Landing, that's very nice in the moonlight . . .

And these people before me at the airport who wait in patient queues to be inspected, they too possess their destinations, even if funerals and divorces await them; their futures are printed on their tickets, and they have paid for them. I have never looked down on any traveller, although I have pitied many and disliked a few; I wish them happier journeys to death than mine, for, after all, their happiness cannot diminish what belongs to me.

It must be that we will all reach the same country even before they bury us in it. That country is named in my passport; in the beautiful Declaration of Independence to which I subscribe with all my heart, and in the Constitution which, no matter that it is now being and will always be violated, remains one of the noblest collections of practical principles in this world. I repeat: My Cold Mountain hides itself somewhere in America.

2.

If anyone can locate it precisely, it must be Hemingway, who knows nature, loves exploration and values accuracy. But in the short story "The Battler," when Nick Adams catches out and the brakeman gives him a black eye, the result is not happy. This fails to invalidate my contention; for if the brakeman hadn't thrown him off, Nick would doubtless have ridden to Paradise! —America contains the entire world, as my President and his soldiers daily prove; and that is why Hemingway can at least triangulate upon Paradise when the narrator of *A Farewell to Arms* hops a freight train in the course of deserting the Italian army. *The one I had seen was so long that the engine moved it very slowly and I was sure I could get aboard it.* How could he have been so sure? He must have had experiences in America. Although he calls himself Frederic Henry, that is only for the security man; his real name is still Nick Adams. So he crawls in under a gondola's canvas and snuggles among the guns. *I lay and listened to the rain on the canvas and the clicking of the car over the rails.* This is what one does on a train. Just as when immediately after an orgasm I find myself seeing in great detail each strand of my loved woman's hair on the pillow before me, and each thread of the pillowcase and the smooth white sheet, so as soon as the efffort and anxiety of catching out has achieved its object with the train speeding up and the yard safely behind me, I become conscious of every scratch on the metal cradle in which

I am hid, and I hear the rattling of the train upon the rails and ties more distinctly than I ever will again. Then what? *You were out of it now,* Frederic Henry concludes. *You had no more obligation. If they shot floorwalkers after a fire in the department store because they spoke with an accent they had always had, then certainly the floorwalkers would not be expected to return when the store opened again for business.* And to take my own more minor case, if in the name of Americanism they bully Americans because we act with a freedom we had always had, then what? Why, ride away toward everywhere! *You had no more obligation,* especially when a train passes over bog-islands, ponds and suchlike snares of gravity; if it ever stopped, the mosquitoes and obligations would come, and necessity would send me miserably in some specific direction — why, I'd be wading up to my hips! — but it refrains from stopping, and so I experience magical ease. The wakes of ducks fan out below me; a goose bows its white neck, undisturbed by me; water rushes past me, blue-brown and windblown; and after awhile it will be gone. And so this novel, which began in Italy, and for most of its life exuded Italian-ness, has now clitteryclacked into Limbo, through which one always passes when hopping freights. *I lay and thought where we would go. There were many places.*

Exactly here the book opens up into solitariness and the flight toward Cold Mountain. The love between Frederic Henry and Catherine Barkley grew out of the character-filled, incident-filled madness of the war; suddenly the story becomes simply and profoundly about the man and the woman. Sliding off the freight undetected, he makes his perilous way to her; and reading this I feel what I feel amidst the hard and somehow granular shinings of tracks and locomotive headlights in a trainyard at dusk. I believe in the American myth that it is both admirable and even possible to devote one's life to a private dream. The probability of failing oneself, either through laziness, incompetence or bad luck, or else, worse yet, through dreaming what one only *imagined* one desired, is terrifying. All the same, *you had no more obligation* to public dreams which dreamed you wrongly. So Frederic Henry comes to Catherine. In Chapter XXXVII, fleeing everything, he rows her across the lake.

I remember driving on night roads in the Johnson Valley of California when it was still almost ninety degrees, the long wide black bulk of a mountain or ridge on one side and lightning on the forward horizon. The road's white stripes reached blackness beyond the headlights, then stopped, but this blackness got continually pushed back by our headlights. We were going Everywhere, the two of us. And when we got to Everywhere, we would lie down in each other's arms. And I remember catching out of Sacramento with an earlier sweetheart, after ducking a Union Pacific bull and hiding in the hot gravel; suddenly we were simultaneously safe and in motion in a lovely old boxcar which sped through the city, making all traffic wait for us, and the leaf-shadows kissed us and it was only her and me. We crossed the river. I had crossed that river ever so many times before, but never in a boxcar alone with *her.*

Frederic Henry's strength and skill are taxed on this watery road as they were on the freight train (to quote the reminiscences of an ex-hopper I met in Portland, *we had to board this train or give up by way of a cowardly and possibly disastrous fall*); but finally he says: *I think we're in Switzerland, Cat.* Now they are safe; now they are in Heaven.

I tied the boat and held my hand down to Catherine. "Come on up, Cat. It's a grand feeling." . . . Catherine stepped up and we were in Switzerland together. He knows they will be arrested, but his sweetheart says: *Never mind, darling. We'll have breakfast first. You won't mind being arrested after breakfast.* Then they are happy, safe, in love and in nature until the very end when Catherine dies. Switzerland is where the freight trains go, so it must surely be somewhere on my continent, as is proved by Hemingway's unfinished novella "The Last Good Country," which grows better, sadder and more American every time I reread it.

In his late boyhood, Nick Adams is running away from game wardens for poaching a deer. Hemingway makes it clear that the American "civilization" that Nick is fleeing from is, while more personal, which is to say studded with individual *citizens,* just as drearily oppressive as my own.*

The journey begins, and we experience the same feeling as we do when we read that other unpublished story about the boy who goes with his father on a train trip far away. Many of Hemingway's protagonists, like their author, can look at a landscape they've never seen before and suspect that it will be good shooting country. Nick Adams knows the foothills of Cold Mountain as only a hunter could. And so he leads his little sister into that same Limbo where there is only him and her in the midst of otherness. (Here I interpolate the glowing light at the edge of the trestle bridge, along with its reflection in the river.) When they have almost

---

*The son of one of the wardens, "the Evans boy," is on his track. I cannot say that I would be better off if he instead of any Homeland Security functionary were my enemy. The Evans boy's malice is knowing and familiar; that adds to its hatefulness; but what if no one troubles to hate me and the result is the same? Wondering about whether the Evans boy knows where they are, Nick gets too nervous to pick berries. I would have been nervous no matter who or what was after me. As for Nick's allies, Suzy the hired girl and Mr. and Mrs. Packard, these people are as long gone as the Evans boy! Hired girls are less commonly native-born in America anymore; and how many postmasters can you find who also run the general store; how many hotel manageresses buy poached trout from local boys? This is one reason why "The Last Good Country" is so compellingly sad.

reached the place where they are going to live in a better dream for a duration whose indeterminateness is underscored by the fact that the story remains beautifully unfinished, they enter the tall and sunless virgin forest, and the beloved little sister says: *I'm not scared, Nickie. But it makes me feel very strange.* Nick replies that he always feels strange here, *like the way I ought to feel in church.*

This must be the night feeling that freight train riders know.

3.

One night not long ago, in a certain desert valley that I love, a farewell gathering for friends had ended, and we were all feeling sad. Since I had been sitting in company for hours, I decided to return to the ranch alone and on foot. It was an easy walk of three or four miles which I had made several times over the years, always in the heat of the day. Now it was coolish, windy, and so cloudy that I could just barely see my feet. Usually the desert nights are star-bright enough even in moonless intervals, and so I had a sense of joyous adventure setting out, with a small bottle of water in my shirt pocket and another in the pocket of my bluejeans. Presently the lights of the departing cars began to stream as slowly as a funeral procession down the dirt in the neighborhood of my left shoulder. I had chosen another road which was shorter and sandier, so that I would have it to myself. When the cars reached the main highway, which it took them surprisingly long to do, they turned right, representing themselves now by the tiniest precious beads of yellow-whiteness, snailed across my vision, and were gone. Then it was darker than dark. Fortunately the sand was pale enough to reflect its soft reliability up between the silhouettes of my feet. I stayed in a rut and walked easily, the dark wind at my back. By the time I had finished my first bottle of water, its contents were as warm as blood. The wind grew increasingly wild, the darkness more absolute. I could barely see the lights of the old maintenance station ahead; the ranch lights were hidden behind those; I recognized the mountains more by memory than by sight. Suddenly I began to ask myself: *Who am I?* I found that I was speaking aloud. Over and over I whispered and shouted to myself: *Who am I?*

4.

The ranch was old, and accordingly verminized in abundance. A fairer way of putting the case might be to say that its concentration of water made it no less attractive to other species than to mine. The season of moths was then upon the place. If I sat reading by a single lamp, with all my doors and windows swelteringly closed, they somehow found their way in, literally in the dozens. Turning off the light and going to bed was the best way to prevent too many more from joining that host, but then they brushed their wings across my face until they were settled, or sometimes flew inside my pillowcase and began munching right next to my ear. One well-informed lady advised me to set out glasses of water for them to drown themselves in, but they did not seem to like my glasses well enough to die in them, so in the end I just let a quarter-inch of water into the bathtub and left the bathroom light on. This worked beautifully. In the morning I could hardly see the bottom of the tub for all the dead moths. Every three or four days, when enough of them had accumulated to produce a stink, I mopped them up, let out the brown water, and let in fresh. Then I would go off to breakfast. Most mornings there would be an eviscerated mouse at my doorstep, brought by one of the ranch cats, and already black with flies. In the week that my little girl was there she wanted to catch every creature she could for a pet. I caught her two lizards and we let them go; she caught a moth or two and then took them outside; she stroked the cows and calves; but what she really wanted was a mouse. The disembowelled mice made her a trifle sad, but their principal effect was to remind her how much she wanted to play with a live one. Once in front of the boardinghouse when we were waiting for the lunch bell to be rung, we spied a mouse between two logs in the sand and she chased it, stroked its tail and generally did an excellent job of being joyous until a man murmured about hantavirus. I was not overly impressed at first, but then in a tone of fear and horror the man informed me that the ranch manager's wife had died of it; they'd exhumed her and verified the case. After that I sent my little girl to wash her hands with soap, and I would not let her try to catch any more mice. She understood why, but her heart did not understand, and so whenever she thought about mice she felt sad.

Some days after she went home, I found among the dead moths a mouse in my bathtub, endearingly formed, with beautiful dark eyes. How she would have begged to keep it for her pet! My first thought was to catch it in my gloved hands, take it out to the fields and let it go. But then I saw that the white porcelain around its tail was marked with blood. What if it carried that deadly disease? So I decided to kill the mouse with the edge of the dustpan. I remember that as I raised that heavy metal blade over my victim, it remained perfectly still, but its front and back legs were stretched out as if it were running. And I hesitated. It seemed so well made that I felt queasy with guilt. But there were ever so many other mice living and dead all around the ranch; and the cat still left one for me every two or three days, always disembowelled and supporting a column of flies when I found it on the way to breakfast. And I confirmed that this mouse was bleeding from no visible wound, so it was surely sick if not injured. But somehow the creature reminded me in its poised frozenness of me myself, waiting and hiding on the edge of a trainyard, longing to leap into my boxcar-hole and be free. And I felt that I was about to do a bad deed. I did it, crushing the mouse on the first blow, making sure on the second, which destroyed the remnants of its beauty forever, its brown silky fur now sodden, disheveled and grey with water, blood and dirt. It lay on its side, as disgustingly shapeless as if it had drowned and gone rotten days before. I scooped it up on the dustpan, not without multiple efforts, since it was disintegrating, then opened the door and flicked it over the ditch and into the weeds. A quarter-hour later the flies were on it, and by the end of the day it was gone.

Who was I, to do such a thing? Aside from any guilt that might accrue to me — although I would have been guilty to let an infected animal go, and perhaps guilty of cruelty to the mouse itself not to end its suffering, if it was in fact suffering, of which I saw no indication (and so because I insist on my righteousness and have not yet done insisting on it, I probably do feel guilty)—there is also the issue of *sadness*; I feel sad whenever I take a life, and when I remember my role in the death of any creature, even years later, my sadness comes back, as it does now; and there is finally the matter of *disgust*: at myself, at the presence of the mouse (not the mouse itself) for putting me in this position, at the sad little corpse which I'd ruined just as the cat would have — surely more mercifully than the cat, but on the other hand, I reasoned my way into doing it;

I chose to do it; humanly atrocious behavior is excusable in a cat on the basis of instinct; in short, who was I? —Guilty, sad, disgusted and disgusting, reasonable, courageous and kind, a murderer who held his head up high.

5.

On another night the crescent moon had risen between the branches of a tree, and presently a small star also shone there. It was so deliciously cool that I lay on my back on the ranch, watching the bats skeetering overhead in an eager hurry and listening to the mosquitoes around me. I had forgotten the mouse I'd killed. I wondered who I was, this time in idle wonder instead of guilt. Who would I become? What would I do before I died? What was I meant to be? How could I better know myself? Cricket multitudes comprised the Greek chorus of my life, whose theme I pondered most luxuriously until just before I arrived at the slumberous essence of things, or possibly after, a huge moth divebombed my nose.

6.

Much later, near midnight, I went out again. The moon was long gone, but the entire tree was blossoming with stars.

7.

On another occasion it was almost sunset, and golden cloud erupted from an almost silhouetted mountain. Who was I? I waited for dark, not knowing why. I looked ahead and the mountains drew my gaze up to the sky. I think we're in Switzerland, Cat. Walled in by mountains, I did not feel imprisoned by them.

It had just rained, and I saw the purple sage, which offered itself to us only in rare years. I crumbled a blossom between my fingers, and the scent nearly made me drunk. The cloud-explosion to the west was redder now, the sky around it more luminous although it was actually losing its light. I gazed across the sagebrush, tumbleweed, saltbush, creosote bush, and my vision was not hindered; it sped to the mountains with my thoughts. Without mountains, would I feel still freer? I thought not, because the mountains led me to the sky but did not occlude it. Indeed their height made the sky seem higher. Now, in an arm of that red cloud, I saw a crescent moon which presently revealed its shadowed part. I wondered who I would have been, had I never been given the great gift of seeing and remembering this. And as I stood here, the question suddenly became: *Where am I?* Was I at the center of anything? Was I above or below? I could walk a mile, or five, and still be in the same place, with only the mountains receiving my sight at subtly different angles. The red clouds were grey now. The glowing sky to the southwest had chilled its color. The neutral yellow-silver of the moon seemed accordingly warmer.

Where am I? What if I am not here because I am not myself?

8.

Here now turns out to be the almost shocking whiteness of the pigeon dung-streaks on the massive black X-girders beneath the bridge at Portland's Union Station, long honey-colored rays of sunset-light stroking the black asphalt of the portico, the clock-tower shining in the melancholy late-blueness of the sky, and the tracks as grubby-black and wicked-silver as dirty razorblades.*

In the light, looking toward the steel bridge, whose silver-white is now almost true white, the rails and ties have become the same rusty red; the evening is fever-hot; the train whistle sounds far and sad, as if it will never be calling me to Everywhere any-more; and a cool grimy breeze blows out of the ribbed black tun-nel while cars reverberate ahead; then the whistle blows away, still far away and out of sight.

Once upon a time, the old marble lobby was lettered to indi-cate the directions: FROM TRAINS and TO TRAINS and toward THE STA◇ MASTER, toward the TELEPHONES, toward the BAGGAGE ROOM; with polished wooden waiting benches as shiny and solemn as pews: —this is a church of the old America! Looking out across the tracks at the late summer trees which now grow ever more darkish-green in the twilight, I longed for my train to *back then*.

9.

Where I should be, and who I ought to be, are mutually determinable. If I were, for example, more energetic and coura-geous, where I ought to be might be in these dry mountains to the east, where years ago I sometimes used to sleep alone beneath the sky. Did I feel that I ought to be there now? Not particularly. I was happy where I was. What did that say about me? Where was my Cold Mountain? How far away from it might I be?

*Talk about the eye of the beholder! One trainhopper I interviewed remembered this yard as "looking like the way station at Auschwitz" thanks to all the lights overhead. He must have pulled in at night, and in fear of the bulls.

Now it was dark, and standing in the knee-high wilderness of desert tufts and shrubs I suddenly felt myself almost *lost.* I was not on any trail. Rattlesnake holes, cactus spines and tangles of brush magnify their difficulty as the night fails. I was still *here,* but soon I would truly have to ask myself: Where am I?

And who would I be, to permit myself to be unprepared for this night, getting lost and chilled? In fact I could find my way back; I still knew the mountains by outline, and anyhow the ranch lights were on. But now everything had fallen into almost one color: the tones and contrast compressed themselves, the sky alone excepted; and soon it too would enter the coherence of the new night. On the pallid sand I saw a lump of obsidian, perhaps dropped here by a Paiute hunter a century ago or more; for that stone does not naturally occur here. I ran my hand over its smooth, almost soapy facets. Its weight in my hand was insistent. I could handle it and experience it, but it kept itself within itself, as did the night which was now a moment away. What if I smashed it with a hammer? What if I could smash the night? Would I see within or between its shards the *hereness* that I had failed to determine in the day?

If I ever could, should I be in the sky? Pale though it was, it still glowed, in contradistinction to the ground out of which definition and meaning were bleeding; and so I wondered whether I ought to follow the sky, going away with its brightness.

And now came the stars.

The valley is a mile high, so that creamy white road of stars takes the breath away. Had I followed the sky away, would I now be there?

Such questions are each as vast and challenging as the North Platte yard, which I've already told you is the largest in the

United States. To answer each of them requires darkness and slowness. Bright speed I refuse to forgo experiencing until the end, but both of its parameters are too great in comparison to myself for me to apprehend it while I feel it. Like an earthworm I need to tunnel through my memories and anticipations of it; like Wordsworth's *spontaneous overflow of emotion recollected in tranquility*. Hence when I ride freight trains my senses open; only later in dark slowness can I try to understand what it is that I've felt. Who was I then, when I passed near Cold Mountain? Where was I? Sometimes I know, but long after the fact. Sometimes I am lonely in my knowledge, but how could I ever feel alone beneath a sky of stars? Tomorrow morning there will be no stars, but if I remember them well enough to believe in them, then perhaps I will know where I ought to be.

10.

Nickie, where we're going to live isn't as solemn as this, is it?

No. Don't you worry. There it's cheerful. You just enjoy this, Littless. This is good for you. This is the way forests were in the olden days. This is about the last good country there is left. Nobody gets in here ever.

Then Hemingway writes the brother and sister into the cheerful place at last, which by the way is also part of the last good country. I am jealous of them. They are at home here, and Nick is an effective woodsman and provider; and he is also, except when he fears that they will be pursued here, happy.

You should have been an Indian, he thought. It would have saved you a lot of trouble.

Hemingway could write that. I never could, on account of that night in Salt Lake when the long train came up to us and kept going, and Steve said: Bill, you can do it! and I thought: If I were five years younger I would do it, and just then the train slowed and I was ready to do it but it was all container cars with nowhere to cling to and by the time the chemical cars came the train was already going faster again. I thought that I could probably do it, but the penalty for failure was high enough that I declined, so that the train went by and I was a little sad, Steve possibly sadder, but behind my sadness there was a coldness; I had become acquainted with my limitations. Had Steve been angry I would hardly have cared. In fact he was good about it. Although he was older than I, he was actually younger since more fit. I could walk in high temperatures more comfortably than he, but he was a climber, a gambler and a hunter. In some ways he was almost an Indian. I was not.

The Cold Mountain of freight train riders must surely be an Indian place. Indeed, the Big Rock Candy Mountain was first of all the myth of the European conquerors, a myth proven by Cortés and Pizarro, who actually found and conquered cities of gold. After that, how could it not be true that more Indian treasures lay hidden in America?

Once when I was in Alaska, an Eskimo woman with a bit of Irish in her said to me: Here in Nome you can drive three minutes and then start catching squirrels, seals, whatever. All year there's always something to hunt. —And I imagined going hunting, with *her*. From Arctic Canada I remembered the alert laughings and pointings of Inuit at a landscape or an icescape; they *knew* it; they were looking for landmarks and animals; they had come to the place beyond Everywhere, the place called Here. To know where the rails go, not just the name but the Here of it, and to still yearn to go there; better yet, to *be* there, in Alaska, for instance, knowing sunlight-haloed manes of dark musk-oxen on golden draws, tundra flowers and berries, melting snow; to know where a shaggy moose is likely to pass, trotting stiffly into the concealing river-willows, to know never to hunt at night, and not to kill coastal grizzlies because they are fish-fed—better to eat the succulent berry-fed animals of the interior—to love Here no matter how familiar it becomes—and with her or someone like her, wouldn't that be Everything?

Not long after meeting her, I was driving down Front Street with a professional hunting guide when a man came yelling exultantly. The guide stopped and rolled down the window. The man cried: Hey, I just saw a fuckin' grizzly up that hill there! Blonde all over, just like a woman! And . . . —The guide smiled gently. They were both happy. They were in Cold Mountain, that moment at least, and so was the Irish-Eskimo woman; and that night I went out onto the street, found an Eskimo girl and . . . Then what? I should have been an Eskimo myself. That would have saved me a lot of trouble. Instead, I got out of bed the following morning, sleepless, thinking: *I've got to get out of here.*

It is eerie how often I come across references to Native Americans among the anti-*citizens* who catch out. A man who camped in sight of the tracks in Sacramento said to me: From my perspective, the Indians were over here, I imagine a hundred years ago, because I picked up a flintstone. —A flintstone! And yet he had to romanticize it, as do I; I have my box of Indian arrowheads, gathered long ago in that desert valley. The Eskimo-Irish woman once found an old ivory figurine buried in the moss. She felt the same about that object that I did about my arrowheads. It was magic; it gave her joy and strength; she would never part with it.

Alabama, the first hobo that Eddy Joe Cotton met, could *put his spirit under things . . . He was just like an old Indian erasing his trail.* Still more explicit in this matter is the guest of the Salvation Army who opines to Cotton that the Indians *were hoboing before hoboing was hoboing and you just can't argue with that.*

Indians haunt Hemingway's work most beautifully in the short story "Fathers and Sons" where Nick remembers making love with his Indian sweetheart Trudy, who in still another story is called Prudy. "Now if he could still feel all of that trail on bare feet." The trail leads to her. Beautiful, promiscuous, unself-conscious and excellent at making love, she breaks Nick's heart and enriches his soul. I think of that first sweetheart I went trainhopping with; because she was a girl I bought her a funnel to pee through, and proudly held the bottle underneath it. Our boxcar crossed the river. She is mentioned in "The Last Good Country," when Nick and his sister agree not to talk about her, the imputation being that he might have brought Trudy to Cold Mountain instead of the younger girl, who had to beg him.

Maybe the only thing I myself ever wanted from the tracks was clicketyclackety quiet. I own a place without a telephone, and because it is in a bad neighborhood I never raise the blinds. Sometimes I sit inside and pretend that I am thinking when really I am doing nothing. Am I in the last good country? Almost, but not yet. When I arrive at Cold Mountain, Trudy will be there, and she will kiss me. Nick will be with Prudy and Frederic Henry with be with Catherine Barkley, and for each of us it will be only him and her, because the essence of Cold Mountain is *aloneness*, and as it says in "Fathers and Sons," looking back to the time of "The Last Good Country" before all the timber was gone: *But there was still much forest left then, virgin forest.*

chapter five

BACK THEN

Back then, said Pittsburgh Ed, they didn't give a shit if you rode the trains or not. But then BN and SF merged. They got the SF dicks, and they're mean. Now what's that town? Indio? Near San Bernardino? Maybe it's San Bernardino. I caught the north swing out of there. I heard that dick beats the shit out of you.

Meanwhile, Hemingway wrote: *But there was still much forest left then, virgin forest.*

And I thought: If only I'd started catching out *back then,* when I was younger. Think how far I could have gone! That slender punk girl Jayna caught out from Sacramento all the way to Québec City. Well, she's hardly twenty. I could have done that, too, back then.

What if Cold Mountain exists nowhere except *back then*?

Once upon a time the Chicago Great Western called itself *the Corn Belt Route,* and the Illinois Central was nothing less than *the Main Line of Mid-America*! Oh, those were the days, all right! Imagine what blue-eyed corn goddesses I could have caught out to *back then*; just think what important places I could have visited on the Main Line!

And *back then,* before the old open-racked automobile carriers had to get walled off thanks to vandalism, a trainhopper could climb into a brand new car, turn on the heater and radio, recline in the driver's seat and even turn on the windshield wipers just for laughs, getting drunk and gazing out at aspens at evening, grey ruffled lakes peering through a wall of slender-trunked trees at the cruel old mountains like strange blades cutting the greystone sky, snow-streaked below as he clitteryclattered across rich green and yellow delicate meadows, raising his fifth of whiskey to toast the gorgeous swellings of the trees that crawled up the bellies of three mountains—

chapter six

I'VE GOT TO GET OUT OF HERE

1.

In Sacramento just north of the ruined battleship-castle of the Globe Mill, the underpass was roofed with concertina wire and train tracks, and a Union Pacific train often sprawled there. Every time I tried to catch out of that place, a security man caught me. Others must have done better, for there were many cardboard beds around there and a hobo hearth made of scorched bricks around dirt, with a board-bench to sit on; I tried again and got cited again. *I've got to get out of here!* I said.

And in Spokane, which years after failing to catch out I revisited on a hot Sunday in my capacity of a sad *citizen,* was hemmed in by evergreen hills and tall old brick buildings so that I could scarcely breathe; I literally itched to get out of there; I am sure that the fact that my wife had expressed her wish for a divorce two days before had nothing to do with the fact that I kept saying to myself: *I've got to get out of here. I've got to get out of here.*

They informed me that a taxi to the city center would cost me twelve dollars, and the cabbie charged me twenty-three, all the while telling me how clean Spokane was, as if he wanted to sell it to me. (Once upon a time, in the year 1934, a man named Tiny Boland rode the rails and concluded: *There was absolutely nothing for us in Spokane.*) That cabbie was awfully clean himself. As soon as I confessed to him that I sometimes rode freight trains, he didn't like me anymore.

2.

I was slowly walking up Howard Street when the shade came, perfectly staining the old facades; and across a wide concrete bridge, a long freight train went past, and then the yellow light blinked and another two Burlington Northerns pulled past; it was all container cars behind them, most of them Evergreen or Uniglory, with a few Hatsu Marine; they were squeaking, scraping and chugging the clouds for the narrow bit of sky which Howard Street allowed me between the parking garage and the tall silent brick building.

When they departed, I was so lonely that I did not even want out anymore; the container cars continued invisibly overhead without imparting any meaning to me; then suddenly they and their sound were *gone,* the sky empty over Howard Street.

I wandered the hot and narrow brick alley-canyons, my gaze defeated by gratings; then came windows all nacreous like husks of sea-things, every pane different, and there was the smell of garbage. Was this all there was to being anywhere? In the alley where someone had written on the brickwork **I HATE MY LIFE,** there came a view of the elevated tracks, and upon them a string of dark brownish-grey BNSF grainer cars. The cars did not move.

In his Kansas City freight journal, Jake Macwilliamson had written in his own italics: *But I just want to get out.* He told me that the first time he hopped a freight was in Portland. —I was pretty bored and miserable, he said. I would just go down to the yard and hang out. There's a mile-long tunnel by my house. I got on one of the largest old grainers . . .

How did you feel?

I was prettty high! Next time I tried it, it was with some friends, and I was down in Hollister, California. We got together one day, put on these godawful clothes and drove down to Salinas . . .

As for Kerouac, he had scribbled: *Who wants Dos Passos' old camera eye? —or Proust's subtleties? Everybody wants to GO!*

That was certainly what I wanted. I hated my life right then.

I got another taxi and asked the driver to take me to the tracks. He liked me so much less than the first driver that he would not answer a word I said. But he heard me, all right: Freya Way went by, followed by Spokane Pump, Pacific Clutch & Brake, Spokane Machinery Co.; and looking down on the rolling tree-lined mountains in uncompanionable silence, we eventually reached the vast yellow sun, almost as powerful as a locomotive headlight. Just before we reached the yard, whose star attraction was Burlington Northern & Santa Fe Remote Control Equipped Unit No. 6140, bright orange, with an American flag (the engine raced like a trainhopper's heart), I saw, heading off Trent, in the sunset, up toward the grain elevator and the long rows of grainer cars on the tracks, a man with a snow-white beard and a dirty blue bedroll and a white plastic sack, a dirty old Father Christmas. I knew what *I* wanted for Christmas: I wanted to get out.

3.

On that creepy grey creosote evening between long graffiti'd walls of trains in Spokane I met somebody's moniker from Tucson, then cold rusty walls, an old rusty car from Saint Marie's River Railroad, a drawing of a hangman between two pulleys, the moniker of the Colossus of Roads, and somebody had memorialized Big Springs, Texas, and Lincoln Grain, Inc. That was almost ten years ago now. In this retelling of what I could with equal probability have read out of the concrete pages of that underpass in Cheyenne or its kindred volume in Salinas, I pause to greet the Barber of Norway, Portland, Oregon; I send my best prayers to 12 Dead Screws; I take note of Lay n Click, Unknown, N Grand Forks, and Opium Smoke 99, who dwells eternally (or until the next paint job) on the same boxcar wall as Detour for Fags 12-90-94. I kiss Lil Girl and wish Buster joy of his accompanying peace sign. The next peace sign has been slashed through and married to a swastika with the moniker of **LYNCH MOB**. Then comes the drawing of a cigarette and a caterpillar, with the caption **WORMALOW; BEND OVER, OREGON**.

That's right — bend over, Oregon! Someday my train will clink away against a cloudy ridge, and I'll get out of here. If all goes well I'll never see you again—

4.

What if all of us want to get out? In support of this hypothesis I cite the underpass wall in Portland whose proclamation to the world commenced with a set of railroad tracks which became infinite-destined arrows in both directions, then said:

```
    B
    E    F.T.R.A.
CALIFORNIA
    R  4     E
    D  EVER D
    O
    G
9-6-88
EUGENE OR
BOUND
BLOW
ME
```

Doesn't that equate to *I've got to get out of here?*

5.

And what if Cold Mountain exists nowhere on this planet, not even *back then,* and what if there is no Last Good Country, either? What if the closest approach to everywhere is merely getting out?

Reconsidered in this light, Hemingway's great novels, which all revolve around journeys, bear ominous witness; for it can be argued that each journey is a quest for death.

A Farewell to Arms details desertion to, flight with and death of the beloved; *For Whom the Bell Tolls* asserts the impossibility of escape even though it beautifully lengthens into fullness the last moments and days of its doomed hero. In both *To Have and Have Not* and *Islands in the Stream,* unlucky sailors of Cuban waters flee domestic loneliness to win death from the bullets of bad men.

Finally, *The Old Man and the Sea,* whose protagonist completes an arduous circle from poverty and failure to the same, with only the skeleton of his once-in-a-lifetime fish to show for it, spells out the paradigm: It was the journey itself, with its hardships, triumphs, puzzles and unexpected joys, that made these books alive in the first place. Their tragedies do not negate that life, but Hemingway is more deeply morbid than most people know, and so they complete it. How could Thomas Hudson, whose sons are dead and whose love is so wrecked that he can hardly even sleep, not get killed at the end? What would have happened had Robert Jordan, whose fantasies of life in Madrid with Maria are the least believable parts of the book, managed to blow up the bridge and still ride away from the Fascists? Why did "The Last Good Country" remain unfinished? The answer must be that Hemingway could not bring Everywhere into a more than temporary glimmer of being. There might have been somewhere to go beyond *out of here,* but even if he found it, he could not keep it. When I imagine him fitting that double-barreled shotgun against his head, I wish for him what I do for all his heroes when they reach their final page: *the sudden feeling of release and freedom when the last caboose whipped past.*

DIESEL VENUS

1.

've got to get out of here. But where did Badger's freight train go? — To his own treacherous Diesel Venus, who had stolen his dog and was sleeping in another man's arms.

It is a long way to the planet Venus, even in the fastest freight train, and it is no wonder that so many astronauts, for instance Badger, meet with delays at the very least. Eddy Joe Cotton insists: *There are two things that put a man on a train—a woman or a war.* The female principle and the death's head do both make their frequent appearance on the freights; I think that a woman's likeness, or at least her breasts, buttocks or genitals, are portrayed on boxcar walls most often of all, because we would rather represent what we want to reach than what we are running away from.*

---

*Here once again I remember Ira the eternally running Montana hobo, grinning meaninglessly, looking away from me, spreading his wrists as if any instant they would become wings and he could fly away from me. I wish that I had thought to ask him to write or draw something for this book.

Let me restate this more precisely: If anything at all is depicted inside a boxcar, it is most often a schematized female shape: hips, buttocks, breasts, legs and cunt. Often one or more of these reifications of desire will be exaggerated, a strategy as old as the Venus of Willendorf.

On the wall of that boxcar that Steve, Brian and I rode out of San Luis Obispo, the woman is essentially a lush pair of buttocks embellished with a G-string. Her legs end at the knee. Her wasp waist flares out into armless shoulders bordered by a collar or haltertop which, coincidentally or not, resembles something rail-roadish on a map. Some distance away on that same mobile metal canvas, a second Venus's meaty thighs gape, and beneath two doughy breasts whose nipples erupt whiskered rays as busily as volcanoes, a monumental slit presents itself, framed by painstak-ingly multitudinous strokes of pubic hair. The artist has even at-tempted to render some labial and clitoral detail. Beneath this fertility goddess the same or another hand has jocularly written: **RED RIVER VALLEY**. (Another name for this place of desire, no matter that it would be topographically inverted, is Cold Mountain.) She hovers alone upon the black-streaked whiteness of the boxcar wall. But just left of the doorway someone has troubled to make still a third female figure, this one crudest of all: nothing but an immense almond-shaped vulva with a fat black stroke running down the lower part of it to be the slit, crowned by two symmetrical slanted strokes which must represent labial folds. From this organ sprout two ludicrously atrophied legs ter-minating in feet like folded flippers. Our artist was wise enough to comprehend the abstractness of his representation; the legs are there for context.

The boxcar that Steve and I rode from Rawlins to Soda

Springs regaled our aesthetic palates with the most elegant Diesel Venus of all, namely, a rounded letter W above a curvy letter Y, the W weighed down with a nipple silhouette at the bottom of each of its two U's.

On the Washington side of the Snake River, on a dark chimney of rock wrapped round in poison ivy, there are ancient Indian petroglyphs many of which represent deer or elk with back-curved antlers; and the reiteration of vulvas upon a boxcar wall reminds me of these beautiful animals represented again and again on a wall of stone.

A man draws a cunt on a boxcar wall. By so doing, he defies his reality, which is the sadness of a bed of cardboard and newspapers in the woods beside the tracks in West Sacramento. Isn't he better off defying it? — Jake Macwilliamson writes: *We'd had food, drink, and what more could a man want? In the company of other men there is often nothing else.* Thus reality. I have read his account of a voyage by freight from Oakland to Kansas City and almost back. In its pages I found neither anticipations nor pleasant fantasies, excepting only the following, which entered his mind in Nebraska: *The few times we saw chicks we discussed the possibility of being approached by some cutie with a strand of wheat tucked behind her ear . . .* Meanwhile, his friend Ukla was *fantasizing of being picked up by an RV motor home with air conditioner and lovely nymphomaniac midwest girls but no such luck . . .*

Women are rare on the freights. Diesel Venus is thus unicorn-rare, more precious than the philospher's stone, and therefore the gross slit that reifies her is as clean as the yellow-grassed hills of California seen from a train on a clear fall day. I have read of a hobo pimping out his wife to other hobos for a quarter a go right there in the boxcar, but this most anonymously carnal incarnation of Venus is surely less likely to be met with than her devotional image on the boxcar wall.

In Thomas Wolfe's uncharacteristically concise short story "The Far and the Near," the engineer on the limited express has blown his whistle every day for a good twenty years to greet a certain woman and her daughter who live in a little white cottage near the tracks and who eternally wave to him *with a brave free motion of the arm*, until finally his many sightings and imaginations inveigle him into the false sense that he knows them intimately. When he finally retires, he dares to set out for Cold Mountain. He knocks on the door. His hostesses' unfriendliness crushes him. *All the magic of that bright lost way* is then indeed *lost*.

As for me, I never got to meet the Short Punk Girlz, who graffiti'd the fact of their existence onto a train I saw in the Spokane yard just before my friend Scott and I were caught and cited. (Come over here, said the railroad bull, crooking his finger through his Bronco's open window. Just to let you know, you're in the computer now. If you ever come back here again, you will be in *trouble*.) Until that happened, Everywhere still beckoned us. At six in the morning, within an all-yellow glow of sun on steel (hand-numbing cold, golden grass and silver gravel; broken signs, dozer and backhoe ploughs, stock steel), a certain boxcar that read **The Monster** bore a picture of a naked woman, and then, far down the train, another boxcar said **BRENDA** and it also said **FANNY** and **RHONDA** and **ROBERTA** and **ELINOR** and **JOYCE** and **LAURA** and **ALMA** and **MARY** . . . Somebody else, perhaps **The Monster,** wrote his own equivalent of that catalogue of female names. What he wrote was: **SNATCHERS OF PINK**. I myself was no snatcher; I was a kisser. If only I could have kissed the Short Punk Girlz! What adventures I could have had on the rails with those Diesel Venuses! Never mind that if they had met me they would probably not have liked me anyway . . .

2.

When Jim Tully took a vacation from hoboing in a town called Bryon, which is to say when he became a mule driver for a dollar a day, he took note of the other workers' conversations and concluded: *Like most men, they idealized women too much* . . . (I am sure that he believed this only because he had never met **Goldylocks 95**.) *The fellow is always in demand who can talk about women among men on the ragged edge of life.* What is idealization exactly? Is it the same as objectification? On the rails Tully met a one-armed hobo who longed for the lovely girl whom he had had when he was in the Philippines. The way Badger spoke of the woman who had abandoned him was as similarly wistful as the expresssion of any other hopeless voyage to Cold Mountain. What did he want from her? He had had her and he had lost her. I doubt that when he had her he felt that life was perfect. All the same, it would be blasphemy not to acknowledge the way that Venus nurtures us all with her diesel-fueled breasts, cases in point being all the boy hobos who were saved by kindhearted whores, fed and sheltered. A lady in her fifties, whom he calls *a lovely woman,* gives Jake Macwilliamson and his two friends ten dollars, *thinking we were impoverished young souls.* A gas mart waitress for her part brings them free food. Badger might have gottten some of these boons from his Venus. Now that he lacked her, she'd become his reason for riding the rails. Of course he was not riding the rails when Steve and I met him. He lay in the dirt on his sodden blanket, letting the trains go by; in a very few more years, if he lived that long, he would be equivalent to the long and slender whitehaired ghost who slumbered in the door of the voodoo shop in New Orleans; before then he might foreseeably resemble the wiry old man I once met on the tracks in Roseville; his cap was pulled down to his eyes and his neck was sunken into his partially zipped jacket; and after I said goodbye to him he vanished between two trains, so I stuck my head around and he stayed vanished; probably he was in a grainer car's rabbit-hole since there were no gondolas or open boxes in sight; he reminded me of a longtime convict whose aspiration was to get by invisibly; and yet who can say that he possessed no destination? These lone men who travel with puppies or whiskey or nothing, they hide their aspirations as they hide themselves. But it may well be that many of them seek a Diesel Venus at the end of the tracks.

In Sacramento I once met a man who stood beside the cross he'd made to mark his dog's grave, in touching distance of his rock-weight tarp-walled lean-to; there was a fence behind him, and then rocky bushy rubbly space right up to the Blue Diamond tracks. He was the one who had found and cherished the Indian flintstone. He was clean enough, and he rested his hands in his pockets, and he did not know how long he would stay. He had already camped here for four and a half months. He said: I get up every morning and that cross is the first thing I see. There's a certain amount of grief you go through here. But you want that freedom. There's nothing more free than bein' here like I am. This is as close as I come to endeavoring to get close to people, right here.

How safe are you?

Well, the train people have a society among themselves. Of course you have stealing. But they won't take your sleeping bag. You have an underground society that's more truthful. You won't have that corporate greed. We watch out for each other's backs. What you will find down here is some of the most artistic, articulate people you can find. I think my approach to this out here, I think that Jesus Christ must have looked at the same problems I do. But how to approach it in the same perspective that He did, that's the problem. I think, well, if they're driving a garbage truck here, well, God will provide . . . You can't live in fear. I'd rather worry about the red ants that's gonna bite me than worry about who's gonna harm me.

Again I asked how long he might stay, and he said: They're not gonna run me off this river.

I asked him if he would ride the rails when he left, and he said he would. I asked how it generally was for him on the trains, and he said: Well, sometimes the boxcar closes up on you if you don't know how to block it up. — I asked him where he might go, and he shrugged and with a smile simultaneously bitter and hopeful said: Wherever there's a cross, that's where I'll be.

But later I heard him murmuring a woman's name.

3.

And at night, by those same tracks, a man said to me: Hey, you know that girl, that movie star with the long blonde twirly hair? Nice tits? Tell her Mikey's looking for her.

The man was squatting on the dark concrete, smoking.

4.

How might the tale have been told from Venus's point of view?

A beautiful strawhaired woman named Dolores,* who rode far more freights than I ever will, rode alone on only one ocasion.

I did it once from Portland to Sac, she said. That was really crazy. On the way up, we had hot trains with six or seven people and we got stuck in Redding, and then we got stuck right past the Oregon border because there had been a fire, and we were starving, but then this hobo who was like the sweetest dude brought us Saltines. But later when I was coming back to Sac I was so scared and tried to look like a boy — here Dolores made a gesture as if to press her breasts apart and into concealing flatness. — I kept to myself, she said. I hid myself as well as I could. But later when I got off in Roseville, she continued quickly, and I felt that she did not want to dwell on how it had been for her just before then, that same hobo was there and I took him back to my apartment and he took a shower. So weird to like hop off a train in Roseville and say hey. So random. I will say that being a girl, if we needed somebody to do it, I would try to go talk to the switcher . . .

Later on this subject emerged again, when Dolores was telling me about her last time riding the rails.

It was eight or nine years ago, she said. That was when I had been travelling with my friend Jenny. We had been travelling through Mexico, and we took the Mexican railroad up to like Nuevo Laredo. We were paying passengers, but it was almost like catching out because there was no room and so we actually had to sit up in the engine and everybody was throwing garbage off the side. And then we took Greyhound from Nuevo Laredo to Houston because we had only had enough money to go that far. Somehow we got to New Orleans. And then we took the train up to Mobile — and you

*She chose her alias, which is required by an outstanding warrant.

know what Dolores meant by *took the train.* — I remember we got kicked off at Hamlet, North Carolina, she continued. And then we hitchhiked. That was really scary. First out of Hamlet this trucker guy picked us up and his southern accent was so thick we couldn't understand what he was saying. He took us way up to the back country and then he went inside to talk to a man he said was his brother. I think they were trying to do something bad. We were hiding in the woods. We could hear them looking for us. Fortunately somebody had given us twenty dollars and so we eventually used that to stay in a hotel. Then we got this one trucker whose name was Slim, and he told us one story about his daughter which was pretty clearly a lie, like when he said the name of the city where she was and it was actually the name of the country, and while I was in the back and Jenny was in the front he just proceeded to undo his pants. He was not even jerking it; he just wanted to get *comfortable,* he said. So we said, you have to let us out and he did.

So then we were like, we're only gonna get rides from families and women. So the families wouldn't even talk to us. But a trucker who kept talking about space aliens found us a ride with this guy. He said: You need a black man to take care of you. And the driver he found was totally cool. But I felt like that whole trip was kind of scary . . .

Thus the tragedy of Venus: Everybody wants her, and so our goddess has become prey.

5.

One fall afternoon in Sacramento I paid Pittsburgh Ed twenty dollars to tell me, among other matters, the story of his first catching out; and he said: Oh, jeez, that was 1980. I caught out of Indio all the way to Louisiana. Goofed off in Amarillo. Or, no, I think it was Houston on that run. My marriage had busted up. Moved all the way to Florida with her. She was a thirteen-year-old runaway. I thought she was eighteen till I took her home to Florida to her Mom and Dad. Turned into a real bitch. Then we busted up in July 1980, so I took off hitchhiking. Went all the way to Long Beach. Then I decided: I miss her; let's get her. Well, so I met two guys in Indio who said: Let's catch out. I didn't know how to do it, but they said: We'll teach you. Just stay away from the railroad dicks. Although I have met some pretty cool dicks. I think K. Falls* is the best. Now Roger the Dodger the gunslinger over there, he's a cool dude as long as you don't fuck with his freights or you're a Mexican. But a lot of dicks do tell me: The freeway's over there; stay out of my yard or you're going to jail. Well, that first ride was kind of scary 'cause of the derailment I'd read about in the paper. The guy who I first caught out with, we went through Grand Junction, Colorado. Then he got off. Two winos were drinking with me. We woke up and we were free-wheeling, moving a string of cars around, slammin' 'em off and slammin' 'em on, *boom, boom!* My head hit the wall of the boxcar, and as for those two winos, they went flying! I said, man, why didn't you wake me up before we came into this humpyard? Well, I stopped out in Louisiana, or maybe it was Amarillo, and hooked up a job with boats and pipes. I always jump off and goof off in a town. Used to be you could jump off and go straight to a slave market and get work the next day. Nowadays, forget it. Used to go to stab labs just to get a little scratch, then head straight for a slave market. They let you do it twice a week. See all the scars on my

*Klamath Falls, on the California–Oregon border.

arms? Otherwise it takes too much time to build your red cells up. Whole blood, now, I think you can only sell that once every two months. Not bad. Cheap high, too: Straight out of the stab lab, suck down a mug of beer, and it goes right to your head! Anyhow, so there I was, and my ex, she sent me a letter and called me everything but a white man. I called her on the phone and said, you don't got anything nice to say, don't even write.

Do you think it's true that most men who ride the freights do it to go to a woman or get away from a woman? I asked.

Well, as you just heard, it was true in my case, he said mildly.

I couldn't help but wonder if Ed's thirteen-year-old Diesel Venus had perhaps been his goal in name only; otherwise why had he stopped in Amarillo or wherever it was for long enough to receive a letter from her? What if Diesel Venus, the goddess who waits for me on Cold Mountain, never existed except *back then*?

How many times have you travelled with a woman?

One, two. They're great for a bedwarmer and a cook and sex and hustling. But, man, all these other guys you meet on the rails, you've got to call them pussy-hungry. I'm tired of getting into fights on that account: Hey, bud, you gotta go; I carry a sawed-off baseball bat in my pack . . .

(As for Dolores, when I asked her whether she had ever had a romantic freight train ride with a lover, she thought awhile, then said: I mean, like when the first time I caught out, I hooked up with the guy who ended up becoming my long-term boyfriend, but it's funny that he ended up irritating me on that trip. He seemed kind of clingy.)

Pittsburgh Ed told me another travelling story in which a woman was mentioned, and it went like this: Chicago yard is the biggest yard in the world: Five miles long and five miles wide.

Been there once. Dick got us and one of my old ladies. He said: Good morning, you're all goin' to jail. I said: Cool, what time's breakfast? He said: Never mind about that. Just come out of there. So I started throwing our stuff out, tryin' to hit him with it, and he had to stand there and take it. I think we'd caught out of Iowa. He said: You all didn't rob no banks down here, did you? I said, if I robbed a bank, I wouldn't be here in a boxcar, would I? — The police checked me out. — Well, if you don't have no warrants I guess you can go. — Railroad workers gave us water and bag lunches after the cops were gone. Then we hit the freeway and stuck out our thumbs.

What was her name?

Donna H———, nicknamed Dirty Donna. She said to me: I'm not with you 'cause I *need* you; I'm with you 'cause I *love* you. But I got burned out with all her whoring. After I rented an apartment for us in Scranton, Pennsylvania, I tried to be patient, but I got tired of her fucking everybody and staying drunk all night. I finally got drunk and said to her: This ain't happening.

And how about your thirteen-year-old? What's she up to now?

She's ten years behind me. She's forty-three now.

So you don't have anybody right now?

I got gal pals but nobody I'm stayin' with. They get too possessive, and when they're on the rag or drunk, no thanks! I'm an I.T., independent tramp.

What's your plan for the winter?

I don't have one, he said. Thinking about going to Bakersfield. You can stay as long as you want. Three meals a day, showers. Big-screen TV. I never had no problems there . . .

6.

And so perhaps the story of Diesel Venus, for all its schematized anatomical grandeur on boxcar walls, can be summed up in the last two words of the following description on the trestle bridge in Sacramento.

You know BONNIE LEE ALL'S FAIR IN LOVE & WAR. You ain't worth fighting for Bonnie Lee this ain't the way it was supposed to end. I loved you deeply & you stabbed me in the back. Shit happens.

chapter eight

A STICK OF DYNAMITE

1.

Whatever beauty our railroad travels bestow upon us comes partly from the frequent lovely surprises of reality itself, often from the intersection of our fantasies with our potentialities — this is nothing more than a cynical repetition of Thoreau's infinite expectation of the dawn — and from love, hope and suchlike phenomena which may well exist entirely within the previous category. These lovelinesses cannot be denied, even if they most dwell on Cold Mountain and *back then*. All the same, the road itself can be ugly, hateful, dangerous. I may anticipate the water of Paradise; meanwhile there is a bitter dirty taste in my mouth every time I drink, because I've touched the water bottle with my grimy hand.

2.

Everywhere is Cold Mountain. *Anywhere* is not.

They don't want us to be blightin' this place, said the man who lived by his dog's grave in Sacramento. —Well, he went on, it's a dump anyway.

3.

From the Barstow yard's barbed wire and pole-lamps, out of which at sunset a trainload of military vehicles rolls over the long trestle bridge at sunset, all the way to New Mexico's grey clouds and snowy ground, snack bags and beer cans sunken in the snowy shrubs, patches of snow on the grass like lichen, the long track curling east and west, Anywhere can be as stinky and creepy as the abandoned building by the Oakland yard, in whose darkness stuffed animals are smeared with feces, and **RIP** repeats itself on the wall, while urine and oil stain the floor. I admit that New Mexico is mountain-shadow country; I know very well that the Barstow yard, seen from above on a desert night, shows its row after row of lights to advantage, like a beautiful woman smiling with all her teeth, and Barstow's almost a dozen tracks cannot but lure us to Everywhere! Sometimes the best views are available only on passenger service; for instance, there is nothing wrong with enjoying a beer up high on the second deck of the Amtrak, gazing out the plate glass window at the long yellow strip of September grass and the blue strip of Bay — how many miles are we from that sinister hulk in Oakland? The long, mellow whistle sounds. Everything is clean: a gull over water, a gull over reeds, sunset over Benicia. One rides dreamily through the Delta marshes all the way to Suisun City, and then the evening fills itself with fields. Well, it's a dump anyway.

4.

A long train sang behind the yellow sky. From the thickets in the hollow, a man and a woman argued, snapping twigs. I found a low sandy place at the foot of a slope of berries and vines, and there I plumped out my sleeping bag, on which mosquitoes settled in masses. The woman's voice, angry and shrill, twisted outward among the darkening trees. I was in the locality of Anywhere, where even Diesel Venus cannot necessarily bestow joy (I remember seeing a certain L.A. Rose invoked on a rusty Santa Fe boxcar in Spokane; and on the side of another car in that yard someone wrote, coincidentally or not, **ROSE LIES**.) And so I thought to myself: *If only I could get out of here...*

The following day, I walked across a rubbly plain which had the same bitter, open, blasted feeling as No Man's Land in the Bosnian war, but the moving multicolored horizon invited me aboard, so I kept walking. Not long after I passed the burned car, a long-haired woman popped out of the trash, shouting: *Go away! Get the FUCK out of here!* Then her man also shot out of the ground, holding in one a hand a hand-lettered NO TRESPASSING sign, and in the other, over his head, a gun. They lived beneath a blue tarp, it seemed. I would have liked to visit their bunker, but the pistol persuaded me otherwise. After all, as their neighbor who lived by the dog's grave had said: A lot of people don't want to talk to you, because they're very private people. It's like if you live in the Everglades. — So I turned around and walked back, now spying other hunks of rubble like flakes of a giant snakeskin. Then I took a friendlier path to the tracks, where I was just in time to see a couple leaping out of a boxcar. Then they picked their way through the hummocky weeds and vanished.

It's a hell of a struggle to be homeless, a man told me. You spend your whole day doin' three things: finding food, taking a bath and finding a place to empty your garbage. You might sign up for a shower at seven and not get in there until eleven. Once they take your bedroll, you're out guess where. We had a guy who died from hypothermia because they took it from him.

Who did that?

Bronco Billy. He's a bad cop. They told my partner, if they see him here with his dog, they're gonna lock him up . . .

The man wanted to get out of here, I could tell. I asked him about riding the freights, and he said: They find an awful lot of dead people. The freights are entirely different now. You really have to know how to ride 'em.

5.

A man lives beside his dog's grave. The freights vibrate by. How many more graves do they pass every hour? How many places are there where one human being pushed another human being out of a boxcar, where half a dozen men raped a woman, where a drunk froze to death or a daredevil jumped off incorrectly? (Don't ever step on a knuckle, said Pittsburgh Ed. I've seen a Mexican do it in K. Falls and they had to call an ambulance. The train jerked and crushed his leg. On a coupling you have to step on top.) In 1932 a freight rider jumps off for a moment and sees blood leaking from a refrigerator car; one of his brethren has just been crushed when they loaded up the reefer with ice. Accidents are one thing; another are the bulls, who used to make you get off no matter how fast the train was going; one boy lost both legs; and a girl remembered: *Riding the rails became an adventure in terror because of the bulls. They beat riders with clubs, rapping their knuckles to make them lose their grip and fall off.* In Jack London's time, when trainmen sometimes got murdered by tramps, the brakeman might pay them back with a coupling pin attached to a long cord, the pin ricocheting back and forth and up and down against the under-carriage where the tramp rode, until nothing remained but meat. Brakemen were also capable of kicking tramps in the face, or knocking them off the train with thrown rocks.

Those times are gone, and a Union Pacific spokesman readily allowed: Most of the folks who hop the trains are not out to get anybody. — He also said: We have maybe one fatality per year on the road, one guy falling short in an effort to hop off or that kind of thing. — Meanwhile the gentle dark man wheeled his bike down into the weeds at the bottom of the levee and took off his jacket. He exhaled beer. He told me about a comrade of his who'd gotten hypothermia: . . . And so he crawled up under a truck on a cold rainy night, and he died . . . — And of course I seen old No Toes, said Pittsburgh Ed. He died. But it was only frostbite.

Some of the stories assault me like angry ghosts, attacking my desire to feel whatever I feel, even my grief, since if I decline to feel it I might forget who or where I am. On the tracks as elsewhere I will do whatever I can to prevent and mitigate painful situations, but it is their very prevalence, and the strength one must build to endure them, that makes me powerful, and likewise makes power-ful my joy. But how prevalent they are! And how much suffering there is! I possess joy because there is money in my pocket. How often pain cries out on the tracks, with no company but itself, no "use," no help—unless a scream is of itself a fractional release or consolation . . .

Once they take your bedroll, you're out guess where. Sometimes I believe that I cannot stand their pain. How do they stand it? They endure it, or not; and they cause it; they hurt each other! I will not forget one trainyard wall's duelling graffiti, one line of which went: **COME & FIND ME MOTHERFUCKER.** As Cinders said to me: There have been a lot of people hurt because of ignorance and drinking and violence.

I cannot stand the pain! I write this and shout this, occasionally referring to my own pain, and then eventually the pain passes, as does all else.

6.

This place, Sacramento, could have been Everywhere. Years later, when my little girl appeared on this earth, I sometimes took her to the river to pursue minnows with her excited hands; no one could have been more joyous than she. And before she was born, when I slept there by the river, light used to bleed so beautifully out of the orange sky; and far away, beneath a star, tree-silhouettes bled a different light. A figure silhouetted itself behind a campfire and was gone. Then someone was throwing sticks on the flames. A low-flying plane's belly-lights became a constellation of jewels. The figure knelt; sparks rose in a column from the fire. On the road, lights spilled out from leaves onto the sand . . .

7.

But do you remember what Pittsburgh Ed remarked about his own Cold Mountain? *It might not look good in the dark. All kinds of critters out there.*

8.

In the dark, in the dark, beneath the power wires of the cricket-riddled forest, people were breaking branches.

9.

When I approach a stranger's camp, I prepare myself for abuse, and the human being who faces me will most frequently express wariness, rage or fear. To anyone who does not know me I must be a *citizen* at best.

The river has fallen so still that I can count every girder on the silhouetted reflection of the Union Pacific trestle bridge, which resembles two wire-breasts in the night; once upon a time, not long before the end of the twentieth century, I rode across this in a boxcar beside my own Diesel Venus, and it was glorious. Now on this anise-smelling night with the bridge looming and dogs barking between its ribs, I decide to keep my distance from those dogs.

On a concrete post near that trestle bridge, one road gospel announces that

**NIGGERS ARE
FUCKING REDNECKS
NOW.
WHERE IS YOUR
WHITE PRIDE?
YOUR BALLS
WAKE UP YOU
SCARED IDIOTS.**

**JESUS
WAS A
NIGGER
SEZ
LOUIS FARRAKHAN**

**A STICK OF
DYNAMITE UP ALL
NIGGERS ASSHOLES
WHITE POWER
<u>THE BOTTOM LINE</u>
PERIOD.**

As a mnemonic aid, the writer has helpfully added: **UPPITY NIGGER**.

Inside an abandoned building beside the tracks in Salt Lake, a philosopher wrote this eternal principle on the wall:

**Fuck
THE
System
Kill
The
JEWS**

Beneath the overpass in Cheyenne, in the self-indicated hobo jungle where I met Badger, the walls were as black with graffiti as the pale hot skies above the tracks in Roseville were with the bird-flocks; and on one wall a traveller wrote:

COMOMEXICO
NOAY DOS
MEXICO viva PatasieMPe
2005

to which another hand responded:

FUCK
<u>MEXICO!</u>

a sentiment annotated by

GO HOME
WET BACK!

which should be read in the context of an adjacent text:

Fuck it all
Fuck this world
Fuck everything that you stand for
Don't exist. Don't belong.
Don't give a shit.
Don't ever judge me.

and if more context about

GO HOME
WET BACK!

is needed, I refer you back to Pittsburgh Ed, who told me: I had two Mexicans get on, and they were sitting on there drinking and I was playing possum, pretending to be asleep, so I heard them say: We're gonna rob that guy. Luckily I had a .32 Beretta. The train was moving at least thirty miles an hour. I pulled out that gun and said: You talk that way, you're out of here. Jump off! — They didn't want to jump, but I made 'em. Never saw them again. That was goin' into Laurel, Montana, from Hellman. I ride alone. I don't ride with nobody I haven't known at least two weeks...

10.

Hobos hate *citizens* because *citizens* turn up their noses at them. And because most of us on this earth travel toward death with people we know, in fearful hopes of mutual aid against the unknown menace of the monstrous Other, we express ourselves in clumps of likemindedness, like the two Mexicans who were going to rob Pittsburgh Ed because he was a stranger and perhaps because he was white; the natural result was that Pittsburgh Ed disliked and distrusted Mexicans:

**GO HOME
WET BACK!**

And coming up the railroad track there were odd places where the air was still warm from the daytime, and there were two black men on one of those places who cursed me and threatened me instead of inviting me to drink with them; I could have wished for

A STICK OF
DYNAMITE UP ALL
NIGGERS ASSHOLES

but that was not my style; instead, I thought: *I've got to get out of here!* and kept walking among the trees, until I saw before me a pale rectangle of a mattress, with a body stretched out on it, perfectly still beneath the sky, wrapped up against the mosquitoes like a corpse; the river was pale like gunmetal, and striped with the silhouettes of tree trunks; after awhile I came to a fire seen *through* a tree like a trail of sunlight, and there was a shopping cart with an umbrella attached to it, and a black woman, very high, was dancing alone by her campfire; she stretched out her arms to me, and when I kissed her I experienced the same sense of space and freedom as when walking over night water on the trestle bridge. I was so happy, not to mention grateful; I wanted to stay; but I could not know who else might be coming, so I kissed her again and again and then again, walking away, seeking a safely hidden hollow in which to camp. *It might not look good in the dark. All kinds of critters out there.* Someone named Jungle had learned that for himself. On the wall of that underpass in Cheyenne, beneath a certain Bull-Dog's moniker (dated 1996), Jungle had drawn three arrows and written:

Fuck You!
Fight one on one
Punk when
I'm sober
Not 4 on a drunk.

The way to Cold Mountain is riddled with ogres, and it was always that way, even *back then*.

11.

It might not look good in the dark. And when daylight comes, I discover that Diesel Venus is gone, the tracks are as grey as grime and the horizon ahead is as white as pigeon shit. Then a stick of dynamite almost sounds good to me, not to blow up blacks, Jews or Mexicans with, but to blast me straight to Cold Mountain, demolishing the wall in Sacramento that says:

**NO BUMS
NO QUEERS.**

chapter nine

A COLD SUN CRAWLED SILENTLY

On the west side of the river, on a low sandy ridge a man with his cap turned backward sat drinking from a bottle; and then dark stinking mud printed by feet human and animal led away to Everywhere; sticks and fallen trees, green murky pool, wailing birds, mosquitoes on fingers situated him in the demesne of West Sacramento; and upon the muck, flattened cardboard, broken concrete block, an old beer bottle, large size, a paint can in the poison oak, creaking wood rendered this place into *here*.

Through leaves, I glimpsed the back of a man pissing; the framework of a shopping cart, almost swallowed by dappling; a flattened pair of overalls, muck-colored, a life's possessions swept into a pile: garbage bags, newspapers, a sleeping bag, loose insulation, paper cups, the brim of a cap, all packed down flat like items in a mass grave.

Overlooking the river I found a cooler, a propane tank with a red hose going to a stove atop which a big open-lidded pot was steaming crowds of orange tamales.

In the next camp there was nothing but matted newspapers and some lucky foam rubber, with trees around and behind. Someone had tied a pink rag around a tree, perhaps to remember Diesel Venus or perhaps simply to identify the place.

Closer to the trestle bridge, which was grander than the one in Sacramento, the shore was scalloped into terraces by the recent flood. A squirrel slowly headfirsted down a tree.

And now from the earth beneath the trestle bridge, humming rhythmically, power announced itself; then through the sunny grating, I received a side view of a silvery stripe: the long train. Now I could feel its growing vibration in my throat. It came over the righthand tracks. I could see the bottoms of the rails, and, between them, blue sky-spaces, off-silvery with blue and brown flashings where the dirt finally rose to meet the train, I spied a greasy dark niche in which a black figure with folded brown arms sat immobile in the dark meditating or watching, God knows what, guardian of that dirt . . .

It never moved during the train's tumultuous passage. The last torn spiderweb sparkle in the sun and a little bell-switch signalled that the train was gone. Still it never moved.

Now on the ledge beneath the tracks I was able to see a woman's blue-tie-dyed dress, drying in the shadows, river-washed.

A siren sounded. Some teenagers were on the railroad drawbridge to participate in its opening. — Come on, said the girls, you're not gonna tease us. — Then the bridge swiveled sideways, and the boys ran across at the very last moment, leaving the girls on the edge to call after them with mournful bird-cries. And under the bridge, the world became bright green water.

The double-decker bridge swung shut. Its sign said: **SACRA-MENTO COUNTY LINE**.

The refugee from Laos was picking hard sour green fruits shaped like almonds. Smiling, he told me of his ghastly life. Now the cloudy twilight had drifted downward like smoke, and there were many crickets and soaring birds. Ducks went under the bridge. Inscribed on the bridge there was also a skull crossed by a hypodermic and a dripping bottle, and the legend **FTRA**.

The rivet-scales and rust on that metal skin, the tracked and trodden sand on either side, rendered the trestle bridge into something like an aged reptile, on which sat three parasites: three of them, hatted, a woman between two men, bleary-eyed railroad tramps swinging their arms at their sides. I wished to drink with them, but I was merely a *citizen*.

Evening alighted on the back of my neck, accompanied by the smell of creosote.

Then on the bridge a sun, glary but cold, crawled silently, flashing — bright and evil, still soundless. Looking between the greasy trestle sleepers to the dirt below where the wooden-legged man propelled his wheelchair along (he swore to me that a grizzly bear had eaten his leg) I saw nobody preparing to catch out; and now I could hear the train and now I could *really* hear it, and I could not understand why I was not catching out; I needed so much to get out of here—

chapter ten

GRAINER ASTRONOMY

1.

The first chilly day had come, not long after we set our clocks back; and then the first grey humid day arrived. Soon the rain would assault us. I was waiting for my San Francisco train-and-bus when the eastbound Amtrak pulled in. It was mainly silver, with blue and orange stripes. The first passenger car was called Mount Shasta. Then came Treasure Island. Soon the train would go; Mount Shasta would disappear. I realized then how badly I wanted to see Mount Shasta from a boxcar.

Steve had already agreed. I happened to mention it to my father on the telephone, and he fell sadly silent.

2.

Who am I? Where am I? I know less and less certainly, if I ever did at all, to where this grassy, shadowy world is rushing. I sit perpetually immobile within my spinning blood, at home nowhere and never anything but lost. The clouds refrain from travelling just now. They hang over the eastward horizon, a long vertebral column of cumuli. I would board them if I could. I want to get out of here! And although the world scrolls past me and the horn of the engine hoots and howls, I cannot get away from here. These short winter afternoons are precious when the sun shows. Shadows and colors gently unravel my desperation until peace comes to me. I live alone within myself. No one can know me. But if I could only get out of myself, *then* I could meet somebody; I could even dwell in this afternoon light.

And who is my father? At seventy years of age he can still outwalk me. Like me, he imagines himself a maverick and is actually a *citizen*. But the security men are tightening their definitions of *citizens* every year. On the most recent time I saw him, they shouted at him because he handed them my mother's boarding pass as well as his. I imagined standing behind my parents in line. I imagine saying to the security men: Please don't shout at my father. — I wonder how that would have ended?

To every man the right to live, to work, to be himself, and to become whatever thing his manhood and his vision can combine to make him — this, seeker, is the promise of America. Thomas Wolfe was the one who wrote that, of course. Who am I that in my yearning for America I cry over and over: *I've got to get out of here?*

3.

That spring at the end of the flood season Steve and I had taken a drive up to Marysville to seek a better spot to catch out than that inauspicious bit of double track which had deposited us back in the Roseville yard. We found a junction, a signal, a long train sitting in the hole (Steve chatted up the friendly engineer) — and a railroad bull who cruised ten paces behind us in his white wagon until we had gone across the highway from his jurisdiction. Accordingly, we figured to catch out at *zero-dark-thirty*.

The rains had already arrived, but three days before our adventure the sky went blue, and two days before the weather continued sunny and crisp, with the fallen leaves both heaped and overspread on the sidewalks like the months of this old year and all the years of my crumbling past — I still had, fate willing, a few new and glorious years ahead; and when a neighbor at the coffee shop who overheard my exultant announcement to Joe the Espresso King that come Friday I'd be riding the rails again said: *I disapprove; I disapprove,* my heart overfilled with glee. Her son had done it; Joe wanted to do it; I was *doing* it.

A few days earlier in that same coffee shop I had asked Dolores how she used to feel about the general public during her freight adventures and she replied: I definitely felt like I was like, why would you pay to fly when you can do it this way when it's only a little bit longer and it's nicer? I think definitely, like on that long trip, I felt like, oh squares, fuck them, they don't understand *shit,* you know. I definitely felt I was like cool for doing something different.

For me it was not quite this way. I have not yet been able to develop any hatred for *citizens.* Nor do I possess pride in my difference. I never rode the rails for financial reasons, or even to get from Point A to Point B—unless the latter equals Cold Mountain.—I guess it was always to get to a certain place, Dolores had said. But the reasons were like, oh, so and so's up from Bellingham; let's go meet her and bring her back down. I guess there is always some kind of destination. I've always wanted to do like the Northern Line . . .

Once upon a time, more than a quarter century ago, a behavioral psychologist offered to administer the Minnesota Multiphasic

Personality Inventory to any of us who were interested. Nowadays I'd surely refuse, because I don't want the security men to know more about me. Back then I wished to know myself. So I filled out the questionnaire in all sincerity, and learned:

DIFFERENTIAL PERSONALITY INVENTORY	Group Mean	YOUR SCORE	Self-Rating	Peer-Rating	Bill Vollman (Name)
1. Well Being	32	10	50	68	
2. Social Potency	48	43	70	52	
3. Achievement	51	93	90	75	
4. Social Closeness	23	13	70	47	
5. Stress Reaction	47	33	70	44	
6. Alienation	45	59	70	50	
7. Aggression	40	64	10	35	
8. Control (vs Impulsive)	27	64	70	52	
9. Harmavoidance (vs Danger Seeking)	29	48	30	50	
10. Authoritarianism	16	5	30	34	
11. Absorption	68	77	60	61	
I. Positive Affect	41	51	70	57	
II. Negative Affect	52	65	50	53	
III. Constraint Acceptance	16	36	30	29	

Mean error in self-rating: Group range 14 to 31 points; Your mean error = 17

Mean error in rating others: Group range 25 to 29; Your mean error = 35

Mean error in others' rating of you: Range = 17 to 36; Your mean error = 17

DIAGNOSIS AND PREDICTION: You will have to learn to control your tendencies toward impulsiveness and danger seeking or you may never become a Trustee. You should try to think kindly of your parents who mean well in spite of how it may seem to you. Your creativity and imagination is compensated for by your athletic abilities. Anyone with your feelings of rejection toward authority had better learn to avoid the fuss (and remember that some of them look just like you these days). There is a short, blond stranger in your future. You will never beat Fred two out of three. Try to make more friends; even Deep Springers aren't so bad when you get to know them. You will be a Leader of Tomorrow.

Short version of Minnesota Multiphasic Personality Inventory, administered *ca.* 1978. If I took this test today, the results would surely be the same, right down to the mispelled name.

As for Steve, why did he do it? Why did Steve do anything and everything? Well, why not?

4.

I mentioned our itinerary to my friend Ben and he said: That's extreme. — He had no desire to do it at all.

I tried to tell him how happy it made me to be with Steve just to keep company with the man's generously cheerful daring. Then Ben joined the army of the silent.

5.

That day dawned foggy-white and ghastly, and I had a sore throat. Oh, well. As the fog rose, so did my spirits. By noon it was cloudy and sunny at the same time. I packed carefully, spending an hour. Evening's livid clouds found me in an almost manic state of anticipation, and by the time I'd wrapped cellophane tape around the two most important packstraps and their mates, so that I could easily redo them in the dark, I felt satisfied and ready. The day had started coolish and went thankfully warmish. I was sweating in my layers of clothes, satisfied to know that I was gaining in my contest of preparation against whatever tricks the night might play on me, always assuming that I didn't get shivery wet. Of course my two liters of water might not last now; my spoiled urban metabolism fretted between too hot and too cold; but I knew that I had done my best. And so I sat happy and ready on the stairs waiting for Steve to appear out of the darkness behind my front door's window.

6.

Steve's wife drove us up to Marysville and not long past seven left us at the foot of the levee, precisely where Steve and I had parked that spring. It was nearly sixty degrees outside. Climbing up the slope, we found Binney Junction and took up quarters behind the switch gear shed, which been graffiti'd with a pitchfork and other insignia of the guiding principle of most human actions. Here we watched the low slime of tule fog eat trees and highway moment by moment. Which track was ours? Steve opened his cell phone and called our secret agent, a disaffected Union Pacific engineer, who assured us that the lefthand track always went to Dunsmuir, which was where Steve wanted to go (I never cared much where we went), and the righthand track led either to Klamath Falls or else way east to Winnemucca. The lefthand track it was, then. The difficulty was of course that by the time a train had evinced a leftward or rightward disposition, it would already be in motion. Behind the actual switch was the only place we could hope to board a nonmoving train. This being reality, there were additional tracks to snarl up the picture: one came or went from Roseville, most likely, and the other one connected to Sacramento. Since we wished to board any available train, we had to be in striking distance of these tracks as well. Because the switch gear shed stood upon a little mound, Steve proposed, and I agreed, that we continue to watch from here.

The fog reached closer, and we began to suddenly to feel clammy. Our backpacks grew wet, as did the ground. Steve found me two flattish rocks to sit on and rushed off about his usual enthusiastic explorations. He returned. Time began to slow down, and I think I yawned first. A goose called like a child. The fog swallowed up all the lower stars, and blurred the next lowest. We could hear more geese. Steve thought that he could see the glints of their wings, but then he wondered whether his eyes were making it up. I had no hope of seeing them.

We gazed ahead at the fog glowing on the horizon.

7.

Steve wanted to check out this track and that light. One of his bon mots was: I'm so fat that when I haul ass it takes me two trips!, but of the many qualitities I loved in him, I most prized his energy. So we wandered hither and thither. Every hour there came a train or two, but none of them were going our way and none of them stopped. Our lack of immediate prospects made us sleepier. We inspected the brightest light of all, which proved to be a security lantern at a construction site, and Steve led me down the slope and said: Are you thinking what I'm thinking? We'd be warm and dry . . . — but I voted against it, because the mesh fence would be troublesome to scale, and might make us miss our train; besides, the light was hurtfully bright and I had no heart to unplug it. So we strolled from one **NO TRESPASSING** sign to the next, taking in night air and watching the trains go by. When they came, we heard their whistles first; then the fog began to glow as if an entire electric city were migrating toward us, and only much later would the spot of glare punch itself out of the mist, resolving into the three-lighted snout of the locomotive. The night continued to be mild and pleasant, so that breathing was a pleasure to me. The fog sometimes had a sooty smell, but more often it smelled simply fresh and rich.

Another train was coming. We strolled rapidly toward the switchbox, but the train never stopped.

Whatever, Steve said.

8.

We sat on our rocks by the switchbox, yawning. For a long time there were no trains.

A shooting star fell whitely and with astonishing speed toward the fog bank and burned out. We both felt happy again.

9.

Drifting once more southward along the tracks, Steve spied a tree at the foot of the levee that he proposed for our sleeping site. To me it was too close to the streetlights of Marysville, but Steve pronounced it *deluxe* because it possessed two not overly soggy scraps of hobo cardboard, rocks to sit on, and, best yet, that tree, a grand old eucalyptus that would keep any rain off. The ground was a soft and dry bed of eucalyptus bark. I had recently bought my little girl a pet lizard, and its terrarium seemed comfortable enough once I had spread out a carpet of wood shavings; so, figuring that what was good enough for a lizard was certainly good enough for us, I gave my assent, and we stretched out. It was around midnight. The night continued to be moist and balmy. The smell of eucalyptus I breathed in refreshed me so deeply that it was like drinking mint juleps. Before I knew it, I was imagining a certain woman whom I wanted to kiss; my hand had just gone home beneath her thighs when a whistling train awoke us. Throwing on our packs, we rushed up that steep thirty- or forty-foot embankment like good insurgents, only to ascertain that the train was a southbound. The whistle fraily wavered, then strengthened almost as rapidly as that shooting star had sped; here came the rush of steel wind! Screeching in our faces, the train flew past.

We descended back to our tree, which now began to drip on our faces. —*Fuck,* Steve muttered. And god*damn* that mosquito. It bit me right on the face. —In pursuit of the next train, we ran up the levee, but the train declined to stop. Walking slowly toward our old observation post at the switchbox, we considered sleeping beneath one of two docklike structures which projected over the far side of the levee, but the grass beneath them was wet with dew and the slope was steep, so in the end we returned to our dripping tree. I pulled my rain hood over my face, and set my thoughts upon the woman I longed for. Her face became a hallucination. I had just begun to suck on her lower lip when a whistle woke us. With pounding hearts we pulled on our packs and staggered up the levee. The fog glowed painfully to the south. Here came our train! It tore past us screeching. — If we'd grabbed hold of that, it would have torn our arms out of the sockets, said Steve sadly, and we trudged down to our dripping tree.

I wanted to go back to sleep and dream erotic dreams about that woman, but I have always been a light sleeper and I had been woken up too many times and Steve was snoring loudly beside me, so I lay on my back, breathing in eucalyptus-scented fog and gazing at a humanoid tree-silhouette atop the levee that to my tired eyes appeared to be advancing toward me; I could swear that it was coming closer and closer but at the same time I was quite aware that it had not moved. Why did I have to concentrate on this tree and not on the woman whose saliva I wanted to drink? I closed my burning eyes. A drop of tree-rain struck the hood of my parka. I opened my eyes again and saw another object on top of the levee which was pale and ovoid shaped. It too was moving and not moving. Unable to decide what it was, I closed my eyes again. How would it be if that woman were lying here beside me in the eucalyptus bark? I wanted to see her, but she would no longer make herself real to my mind's gaze. The fog was now so thick that I could no longer see the top of the levee. Far away I heard the noise of an idling engine. Steve slept on. The engine groaned and groaned. I heard a staccato hiss of compressed air. Could it be a train? Steve looked happy in his sleep. When it comes to trains, I know enough to doubt myself, because, as Badger said, *no one's* an expert on hopping freights! But my ears have always been more acute than my eyesight, and it certainly sounded like a train. Finally, hoping that I was not waking him in vain, I touched Steve on the shoulder. With groggily patient skepticism he strapped on his pack, and we went up to the top of the levee again. I was in a hurry. Steve walked slowly behind and on the ballast. I stepped on the ties of the single track.

Maybe we should pick up the pace, I said. It would be a shame if we missed it. If it really is a train. What do you think it is?

Could be factory noise, Steve said.

I heard the hiss of air again. Steve did not hear it. Doubting myself, I went forward toward the signal light, with Steve trailing ever more slowly. I was doubting myself and feeling very guilty now. Slackening my pace to be at his side, I wandered toward the signal without any hope.

We passed the signal and then a motionless glare of light in the fog revealed double track.

I see it, Steve said.

I did not, but we kept walking, and after a long time, which must have been five minutes, I too could see a locomotive's three eyes.

Got any cigarettes? someone called up to us from the below of the levee.

There might be as many as twenty hobos waiting for a train in Jack London's time. In *On the Road* the hobos are often in the background, for instance sitting around fires on crates in Bakersfield. Kerouac's alter ego notes that *when I looked out the window I suddenly saw an SP freight go by with hundreds of hobos reclining on the flatcars and rolling merrily along with packs for pillows and funny papers before their noses, and some munching on good California grapes picked up by the siding.* In my time there was almost nobody. (Dolores said: I feel like we would just never see hobos that much, to be honest.) I had expected my travels to be picaresque, teeming with wise, bizarre or menacing outlaw characters. At the very least, I had imagined that without really trying I would meet dozens of people of Pittsburgh Ed's sterling caliber. In fact my various odysseys were haunted by absence, with only here and there a few lost voices such as Cinders's or Ed's singing about the way things used to be *back then,* as if they were crickets who had inexplicably outlived their summer. In this account of my journeyings with Steve, I have omitted none of the people we met. This unknown man who wanted cigarettes in Marysville, he was the only soul we encountered in that particular adventure.

Steve asked him if he knew which trains went where, and he did not. He must have been no boxcar-equestrian at all, but a specimen of the weed-sleeper genus to which I have on rare occasions temporarily belonged. Desperate not to miss our freight, I kept walking, and Steve finally gave up trying to pump the fellow for information.

Now we were on the double track and coming into the light. Steve had proposed that we approach the engineer of any train we saw and ask his destination, but, as always, I preferred the strategies of rats and cockroaches. With my black balaclava around my face and my grey-hooded head lowered, I walked into the headlights and passed the engine, pretending childishly that if I did not look up into the conductor's gaze (we were passing on his side, the left side), then he could not see me. I did not look at Steve to see whether he waved, and later he told me that he had not. Of course they must have seen us. But now we were safely past the first locomotive. There were two more units behind it, and I asked Steve whether he wanted to hide on one of those, but he thought that the lights of this small yard were much too bright to cover that misdemeanor, so we kept going, too slowly for my taste; when I am about to board a freight my method is to rush to the first halfway safe riding-place I can find, before the train departs without me; while Steve, more confident in his ability to grab the right car as it passes by, takes his time, and, truth to tell, pleases himself by provoking fate a trifle.

You know, I said, I really think we ought to pick up the pace.

I forget what Steve replied.

There came a whistle, and to the south the fog began to glow. Steve and I tucked in against our train as the Amtrak, presumably the Coast Starlight, came screeching past us, literally close enough to touch. *That* engineer must have seen us, too! I could spy a few passengers through the lighted windows, but since we were literally and figuratively in the shadows, I doubt that we made an impression on them. The final car whooshed by, and I was more impatient than ever to board our freight, because it might have been waiting only for this other train to pass. How much time did we have?

We trudged on, and after the units it was all floorless container wells, and then chemical cars without decks, and finally there was a grainer but Steve didn't like the look of it, and then there were more deckless chemical cars; there came a grainer, followed by a grainer, and I said: How about this one?

Well, if you like it . . . Steve said with a yawn. Anyway, this looks like a junker train. I bet it will sit here all fucking night.

We clambered up the eastern ladder onto the rear platform of the grainer, which was spacious but not discreet, and then valiant Steve proposed, as he always did, to scout rearward in search of an open box to sleep in. As always, I accepted his offer with thanks and a plea not to be too long in case the train started moving. He handed me a piece of cardboard from the tracks and told me to wave it if need be so that if he were running after the train he could spot our grainer from a distance. Then he strode off as bravely as a matador.

Air hissed suddenly in the train. Then it stopped.

I awaited Steve with my heartbeats as sickeningly percussive as the slams of a humpyard locomotive shuffling cars into a new string. He did not come and he did not come and finally he came, saying that he had walked as far as he dared but found nothing rideable.

But we could try one of those units, he said.

I thought you said that it was too bright up there.

Well, then how about that other grainer? We won't have as much room but it's less exposed.

How far is it?

Just one car up.

Steve, I'll do whatever you say.

Then let's go.

He was already down the western ladder. I threw down both our packs and he was carrying them before I could get to my own.

We ran through the gravel to the other grainer. As always, fine and gallant friend that he was, he motioned me to go up the ladder first.

It was the sort of grainer platform with a V of metal ribs ascending around the hole. Beyond the ribs, a narrow ledge spanning the back edge of the grainer sufficed for one human being to stretch out. On either edge there was a ladder at the corner; the rest was a lip not much more than a foot high. Steve tucked his pack into the V and stood waiting for destiny, while I sat on my pack with my back against the wall and my right knee almost overhanging the lip on the western side.

Almost immediately after we had taken our places, air hissed in the train with the sharp loud definitiveness which meant that we were about to go. It was about two-thirty in the morning.

10.

Silently the freight began to creep forward. Then our grainer jerked and slammed, and there was no more silence. I had for once remembered to bring earplugs in my breast pocket, so I screwed them into place, pulled my balaclava and hood back around them, and was ready to ride toward Everywhere!

Steve and I clashed our gloved hands exultantly together and grinned.

We rolled out of the bright trainyard and entered the wide dark world. Black trees sped by.

Watch the track, Steve shouted into my ear (I could barely hear him), and we both stood gazing down between our car and the next into the space where the cruel silver wheels turned in a blur, reflecting each other in each other, and the track unrolled rearward a few feet below us. Now we were past the signal and now we had left our dripping tree behind forever, and here came the brightly lit construction site where we had decided not to sleep, and gazing over the edge of our grainer we saw single track and single track, and as we came into sight of the pioneer cemetery, which was lit up with ghoulish sentimentality, two sets of tracks came into being, gently parting ways, and we took the rightward track, at which Steve screamed: *Fuck!*

I didn't care where we went, so I laughed.

11.

Here I should mention that Steve had brought his collapsible fishing rod once again because he wanted to go to Cold Mountain, which for him happened to be, among other places, Dunsmuir, California, where his friend Jim ran a fishing lodge where Steve and some of his fellow anglers stayed every year. It lay right across the Sacramento River from the tracks. Steve's wish was that we would jump off the train and proceed in grand style to Jim's place, which would now be peacefully uninhabited. Jim had promised to meet us there, let us stay overnight, and drive us to Redding the next morning so that we could catch the Greyhound back.

As for me, all I'd imagined of this ride was us going north and hence gloriously away from the Central Valley's low yellow hills like a chain of fuzzy breasts, hills golden where the low sun warms them, greenish and bluish where it does not, hills rolling restlessly up and down like a long frozen wave and therefore most lovely in the cool of a summer evening; away from them we would be rushing toward an Everywhere that is the antithesis of summer evenings. And why not? It was now almost Thanksgiving.

All the same, on account of my simple equation of freedom with summeriness, my fantasy of Cold Mountain had fallen out of season: Somewhere ahead there would be a cool blue noon of blackflies and aspens, a river running somewhere, globular leaves changing between yellow and green as they trembled; I suppose that it was so far north that it must have been in a country beyond winter where Cold Mountain invited me to live forever.

I loved the fact that Steve went trainhopping with a fishing pole. I enjoyed telling people that he would be fishing out of an open boxcar door, perhaps for fish, perhaps for people's hats.

Now he looked sad to miss Dunsmuir, and I felt sorry.

12.

The black river-sheen paralleled us on the far side of the levee. In the deeper darkness beyond it there were a very few lights. Who was up so late at night? Or did they always keep their porch lamps on? Anyhow, we left them behind; we were going northward at last!

After about half an hour we pulled into the Oroville yard, and Steve lay flat while I bowed my steel-grey hood against the perilous light, but no bulls came. The train stopped. There was a hiss. — Oh, shit, they've cut air! said Steve. Must be a crew change. We'll probably be sitting here all night.

An instant later we were travelling again. An instant after that, we were back within the great world of the night.

Pale lakes or fields accompanied us for a time. The night was so moist now that the breath glowed whitely from my mouth. Relieved to have caught this train and proud to have been helpful in that, I relaxed, and grew tired again. On that account I distrusted my perceptions and judgments. That low steel lip against my right thigh frightened me for the first time. I worried about rolling over it in my sleep, which of course would have been fatal. Since there was only room for one person to lie full length, I invited Steve to do that and decided to stay up awhile. The truth was that because I knew with all my heart that this night would never come again — a fact which I sadly lacked the capacity to apprehend in relation to so many of my other nights (and here I remember Brian saying to me of our ride from Salinas to Santa Barbara: *That night is etched in my brain*)—I could hardly bear to miss a moment of it, and so, sleepyhead though I was, I did not want to sleep.

And how happy I was!

Steve closed his eyes rapidly, and I was riding, thinking my own thoughts but not lonely, thanks to his sleeping presence, toward either Winnemucca or Klamath Falls. Thanks to the fog, there was less to see than there had been on that night that Brian remembered, but there was no less to experience, although telling you what happened to me will be more challenging than relating the sights of that ride with Brian and Steve. Although I sensed river, I could no longer see it. The clamminess of air suggested water; of course the roar of the freight prohibited me from hearing it. Very occasionally black trees filed close by like soldiers on a recon mission. Mostly it was black, and then blacker.

I wish I could convey what a pure and good experience it had been to see that shooting star in Marysville. Now from the blackness I began to see other stars, right over that foot-high strip of steel that reminded me not to fall into Anywhere. I sent my hand an inch over the edge and touched cold wind. I touched darkness.* And beside me there came more and ever more stars, brighter and whiter and clearer than I had seen in a long time. Indeed, I had forgotten the stars, as I so often will on those other nights of my life. No matter what I have accomplished and whom I have loved, how much I have lost by missing the stars for so many of my nights! And now I am grey, and who knows when I will die, and never see the stars again? Who would I have been if I could have been alongside these stars always?

The Big Dipper was following me in that wide cold window through which I could have leapt to my death. I must be in the sky now, for the Big Dipper to keep me company! And that was truly how it felt. When Brian, Steve and I beheld those porpoises leaping under the moon, our joyous awe had approximated what I felt now. I was riding through a river of stars. And I felt as happy as a child opening Christmas presents.

13.

The more stars there were, the colder it got. The next morning Steve would show me on his map of northern California how we had ascended the Feather River Canyon. He had done it once in the daylight and was sorry for me that I had not truly seen it. But if I had seen it under the sun I would never have seen those stars.

---

*To what extent is a freight train a house, a shelter from the night? Just then it felt more like a stage in night's infinite theater. I had no shelter, infinite freedom and ultimate consequences.

14.

We passed through tunnel after tunnel, and the tunnels grew longer.

15.

Dawn found the freight train stopped in a long curve cut into the Sierras. White mist in the treetops, then evergreens going down and down into the gorge announced that we had arrived at Cold Mountain. There was a patch of frost on the deck of our grainer. I was shivering. Steve had pulled out his sleeping bag and was hidden inside it. Had he been awake, I would have asked him, since he had ridden this route before, how soon we might hit Portola or some other dangerous trainyard, because it would be disastrous to be trapped in a sleeping bag with my pack open and my shoes off if we came into observation of the bulls. But he was not awake, and I did not have the heart to disturb his sleep. So I sat there shivering. Kerouac wrote that in Cold Mountain's poems the fog never departs, which made him admire the poet's hardihood. As for me, the steel chilled me through my clothes no matter what part of me touched it. Finally I admitted to myself that I was losing heat, which was, after all, potentially worse than being arrested. So I took off my shoes, stuck my feet and lower legs into a big rubber bag that I had and wadded my sleeping bag around me and over me like a blanket. It was a goosedown affair which had been quite fancy twenty-seven years before. I had gotten my father's money's worth out of it, and the zipper was broken. If I had to abandon it to escape the bulls I could do so without regret, but what if I needed it immediately afterward?

I felt warm now. I drank some whiskey, drank some water, ate a sausage. Then I grew rather satisfied with myself.

We were moving again. We passed through Tunnel Number 2 and arrived in an even higher brighter colder place. Far away across a gorge whose bottom lay far below the mist, evergreens jutted, and through them a track had been threaded, and upon that track rolled the rearward portion of our supernaturally long train.*

16.

Steve awoke, packed up, wearily studied the direction of the sun, unrolled the map, which jittered and chittered in his gloved hands so much that he could not read it, shouted something into my ears which I could not hear, and looked glum. I gave him a smoked sausage, and he munched on it sadly. When the train slowed slightly to round a bend, the noise diminished sufficiently for him to scream into my ear that he thought we were going to K. Falls, not Winnemucca.

We screeched across a high, densely evergreened plateau whose rocks and shrubs were snowdrifted around. The sun caught blue shadows on the snow and made it sparkle as if it were wet. Presently the morning strengthened sufficiently to gild two sharp-angled zones of our grainer platform. We stood up, warming our gloved hands and booted feet ecstatically. Finally I undid my hood. It felt like getting naked. The evergreen air was as good as breakfast, but for dessert I ate some salted almonds and a piece of chocolate. I saw a highway and then a sign for the town of

---

*By some miracle I finally got to see its end, adorned by the red light of the Flashing Rear End Device.

Westwood—information which I shouted into the side of Steve's head. He found Westwood on the map. That was how he confirmed that we were Klamath-bound. I could tell that he was still sad to miss his fishing. As for me, on this cold and lovely day I lacked all goals and disappointments because we were already Everywhere! It was as if we were travelling into one of those Union Pacific picture-calendars that my grandparents always used to send our family for Christmas (for here is as good a place as any to confess that my grandfather was a machinist for that railroad); I remember each month's colored image of a perfect train or locomotive posing in a perfect American scene; and now I had achieved placement on one of those pages. On this ride I had expected to find myself once more remembering with longing the woman in Oregon who had wanted me to *play the game a little*; if Steve and I rode far northward, we'd reach the Columbia River Gorge's blunted bluish mountains, the cold river-crags like teeth, pale reflections and cloud-whites in the water; I had been there with her; she and I could surely have reached Cold Mountain if we'd only caught out together *back then*. The fact is that I never thought of her. To be sure, I was stupid with chill and sleeplessness; perhaps I should have imagined her; but I truly wanted for nothing; I did not miss even the Columbia.

Steve thought that we would reach K. Falls by nightfall. He'd been kicked out of that yard twice. Once he and his buddy were playing ball between the tracks when the bull caught him; that sounded like Steve, all right. We bulleted higher into the warming day. Eight hours after we had caught out of Marysville, I spied a hand-painted sign at a forest siding that said **WILLOW JUNCTION**. Steve could not find that metropolis on his map. But then there came another landmark: a pool of cloud on the horizon below us from which rose the top of the gloriously white, white pyramid of Mount Shasta.

Shit, said Steve. We're so close to Dunsmuir!

And then the train stopped.

Steve rushed off, dwindled on a ridge — I was wondering what to do if the freight started without him — and then he came strolling happily back and said: There's a road down there! With traffic!

So you want to get off here?

You bet! Right here in the middle of B.F.E.!*

Are you sure?

I'm sure. If it wouldn't screw up your book—

I threw our packs down into the moss and clambered down the ladder. It felt wonderful to be in motion. I had not realized how numb my feet were.

There was a lonely feeling when the freight slowly began to depart, and we stood in the delicious sunlight, up to our ankles in lava and weeds, my ears still ringing from the train—which reminded me to take out my earplugs. And then our freight, which only when Steve pointed the markings out to me did I realize was a Burlington Northern, increased its velocity and was suddenly *gone*.

We walked down a muddy track, came to road, hitched a ride, ate breakfast at Chatty Kathy's, and lay down in the street to snooze until Steve's friend Jim came to get us. I slept in the backseat all the way to Dunsmuir. Then I lay down on top of the bedspread in a cabin at Jim's lodge and slept all afternoon. As for Steve, he rushed straight to the river and caught three trout.

---

*One of Steve's favorite abbreviations. It stood for Bum-fuck, Egypt, and meant "No-wheresville."

chapter eleven

LOST AND FOUND

1.

Montana Blackie, whose official biography is called *The Last Great American Hobo,* used to have his camp in West Sacramento, on a stretch of river that I first visited nearly a decade after the police had run him out. I never met him, but the book he inspired is beautiful. He gets quoted as saying that he chose not to be a *citizen* because *it's like my friends, who work forty years at the same fucking job, then they retire and six months later, they're dead . . . They want to keep up with the Joneses. What are you showin'? Why the hell do I gotta compete with that guy over there?*

So he refrains from competiton. Better still, he follows Thoreau's admonition: *If you have any enterprise before you, try it in your old clothes.* His shanty, which cost even less to build than Thoreau's, is a marvel of organized simplicity. His skillets hang all in a row; he has his dog, his friends, the pornographic magazines he scavenges from dumpsters, his seclusion and his river view. Has he reached Cold Mountain, then? Should I emulate him?

His biographer and photographer, who as much as I do loathe the unfreedom that is creeping over America, discuss this question as it relates to themselves. The biographer concludes: *We lacked that something in us to do what Blackie did long ago . . . becoming a hobo goes far beyond dropping out. That something is part strength, part weakness, both pure freedom and an absolute prison.*

As for Thomas Wolfe, that lover of trains, journeys, quests, chance-seizing and wild liberty, the most common word he uses to describe hobos is *brutal,* although he might grant one of them *a curious nobility* should he happen to exemplify *a legend of pounding wheel and thrumming rod, of bloody brawl and brutal shambles, of immense and lonely skies, the savage wildness, the wild, cruel, and lonely distance of America.* Usually Wolfe reads no legend whatsoever into the hobos' faces. Typical is his account of a low-class whorehouse in Newport News whose clients are mostly *foul, filthy, wretched, hungry, out of luck, riding the rods, the rusty box cars of a freight, snatching their food at night from the boiling slum of hoboes' jungle.*

And do I want to be Ira, or Badger, or Sheldon? (If there is wisdom to be met with on the road, does it come from one's fellow human beings?) The first of these track-riders was haunted; the other two were lonely. Well, so what else is new? A hobo from 1932 remembers that *you were always with people on the trains* but that *everyone on the road was lonely.* The hunted lonely sweetness of Sheldon was quite probably superior to my own being, but since when did I and all my worldly brothers and sisters ever envy Christ?

I used to be a machinist, back in the seventies, said Pittsburgh Ed. That was good pay. Makin' bulldozers and all that stuff. But I was too wild . . . — There might have been regret in his voice. I scarcely envied *him.*

I inquired what had been the most memorable thing that had

happened to him on the rails, and he said: A friend of mine years ago, the wheel jumped the track right in front of the grainer he was riding. He said: I'm gonna stop this train! Took his knife and cut the airhose. That stopped it, all right. They had to get a crane to get that train out of there. The engineer was grateful; that saved the train from a derailment.

That story was not entirely incredible. It reminded me of the glorious finish in *The Road* when Jack London wins the admiration of the firemen, and even the brakemen say: Well, I guess you can ride, Bo. There's no use trying to keep you off. — Maybe it was even true.

I asked Ed what he was up to just now in Sacramento and he replied: I caught out from Bakersfield to here, four years ago. Caught out one night, stopped in Fresno for about five hours, got off here about noon. Reason I came back is, I did placer mining in Colfax in '81, so I told everybody I'm goin' back to Placer County to die. I'm gonna rephrase it. I'm gonna do that *until* I die.

That was not such a bad answer. But then why was he drunk in the street the next day, his face oxide red like a boxcar?

It is certainly not living the life of a *citizen* who has been hoodwinked into wasting himself on trivialities that I fear. *Why the hell do I gotta compete with that guy over there?* I never have. Actually, I like *citizens.* My neighbor at the coffee shop who said of my freight adventures *I disapprove; I disapprove,* I swear that she never offended or humiliated me. But the lady at the bakery who told my father that he must stop blocking the line *right now*; and the hotel clerk in Cheyenne who required identification before I could insert my plastic key in my plastic door; these *citizens* are the dependent children of security men. It is the security men, the necessary evils who make each succeeding year of my life more unfree than the one before, these are the ones whom I hate and fear.

But I remember one night in San Francisco's Chinatown, smell of fish-ice on Grant Street, smell of oil, smell of pork dumplings, and the silhouette of a fetus curled in one window, smoking a cigarette: — Who was this being? Was it living or dying? It snored as it smoked, huddled in a puddle of melted fish-ice; I could hardly get that smell out of my nose . . . And I remember the couple who slept below and on the far side of my wall in the dirt and grass of San Diego one early morning in a galaxy of luggage, including a far-flung hat and open book. They might have been trainhoppers; they were most definitely migrants; they lived the free life, perhaps, but I pitied them; never mind whether they pitied me.

And once again and yet again I remember their opposites, the *citizens* about whom Thoreau sadly inquired: *Why should they eat their sixty acres, when man is condemned to eat only his peck of dirt? Why should they begin digging their graves as soon as they are born?* My darling America has become a humpyard where cars and *citizens* can be nudged down the hill onto various classification tracks. I've got to get out of here.

So what do I want? All too soon I will aspire to retire into a fortress so that my life can go safely by. I have been digging my grave from the instant I was born. Well, I definitely want to get out of *there!* I want to catch out for the stars, but in an Illinois Central steel caboose from the 1960s, with glossy, dimpled cushioned benches, a coal stove venting through the ceiling, a steel sink, a water closet in its own compartment, a grab iron along the ceiling; everything wide and comfortable and steel-grey in the old black-and-white photograph, adorned with light-gleams on walls, ceiling and floor.

The man who camped by his dog's grave had said: There's two types of people on this railroad. One type is the type with nothing.

Then there's the second type. They're here because they wanna be. — I wished to belong to the second type. But what if I can't get out of here unless I became one of those with nothing?

Who am I? Where am I? What should I carry with me? Should I run away from *back then*? What if all memories or resources are merely train ballast with snow on it? Certainly I will someday resemble these bits of a dead dog I've seen near the boxcar wheel. On Cold Mountain grey clouds are shingling the cold roof of sky, and he who forsakes Plastic America receives in exchange a corduroy sky of slanting rain.

2.

Well, but I was not the only rider who wished to live easy. Jake Macwilliamson's party from Portland used a cash machine on their long freight train ride from Oakland to Kansas City, Jake remarking: *Such luxury for a group of poor old hobos.* After a bona fide hobo had kept them company for a while, first guiding and then bullying them, Jake was relieved to see him go. (Met up with him in Lincoln, Nebraska. We were sort of at our wits' end, and he took us under his wing, he said. But then he started to completely spook us out. We were having visions of pushing him off.) After all, Jake was a *citizen* like me.

3.

Once I asked Steve to tell me the most beautiful experience he ever had on the rails, and he said that when he was younger he and a friend were riding through the Idaho Panhandle. There were still cabooses in those days. The two men decided to take the second to last caboose, since a conductor would surely ride in the last. Steve left a note for him which said: *We are two college kids catching out. Hope that's OK. If not, let us know and we'll leave.* Then they hid. The train began to move. Steve and his friend stood up. The train man was in the last caboose, doing paperwork. They waved to him. He strode across the coupling and said: Got your stove going? — Oh, we never touch anything on the trains, Steve assured him. — Well, then, let me start it for you, said the man, and he did. Then he left them to their travels. Steve said that there was a viewing turret in that caboose; he and his friend went up there and enjoyed the scenery. *Such luxury for a group of poor old hobos.*

4.

Dolores thought that she had been about seventeen the first time she caught out. She told me: It was sort of the punk mode of transportation, really. All these people were going up and down between Portland and California. The first time I did it from Eugene down to here. But nobody knew what they were doing. But then that feeling of like total amazement, when you're up in those Oregon mountains, in the clouds ... —and she smiled the ecstatic Cold Mountain smile.

I think it was like me and three other guys that time, she said. Then I took a longer trip with one of my best friends and two other guys, and we went from Portland to southern Nebraska. I got a warrant still, a trespassing warrant. We got kicked off at Lincoln. Since we were just kids, everybody thought we were runaways at that time. They gave us a ticket with a court date. Of course we didn't go. That was the only time they ever did that. God, that trip had to have been probably at least four days. It was

n't the yard in south Chicago,

thing, it's getting to the yard.

ck enough food, you know. We

od! At the same time, I remember

nothing out there, you're not

wide open feeling . . .

face again and she said: Really to

the one between here and Portland,

is really gorgeous.

the South and that's, like, gnarly.

In the middle of summer where you're

nan. We did it from New York to Mo-

bile, Alabama; it was me and my friend Michelle and two
guys. That may have taken at least a week. We were stopping in
small yards and then we'd have to change trains. A lot of times
people would see us and they would give us fast food; we looked
so pitiful. We stopped in like northern Florida for awhile. Maybe we
got kicked off in Georgia; it was either Georgia or Florida; we were
trying to hitchhike and the cops stopped us and said: We will
give you a ride to the next county, and in the next county the cops
were waiting to take us to the county after that.

When I asked Dolores her favorite part of the train to ride in,
she replied: I always liked the grainers.* The boxcars are nice. You
have that freedom to get up and move around in there. An engine,
yeah, that's pretty sweet. There's like water and food. But I always

---

*"Back end of a grainer," said Pittsburgh Ed. "It's wide open. Well, I've been on the front
of a forty-eight before when it hailed like a sonofabitch and the hailstones were *this*
big!" — "Well, the back end of a grainer's nice," said Jake. "A boxcar's okay for doing a
short run. A container train with the three-foot well's not bad; the corrugated ones with
the indents always have a well . . ."

like to be outside. When I was outside I was on a piggyback, and I was trying to hide under the wheels; that was kind of crazy; well, anyway, I just like to be outside.

Most of the time we would get off when it wasn't moving. There was a few incidents like where my friend who was really short tried to catch one out of Portland and she was like falling. The train eventually stopped and the bull came up to us and said: We watched the whole thing. But then he said: Just lay low and get back on. — On the other hand, we found out about this accident which one person we know was in. They were riding from Sac to Emeryville. I don't think they knew what they were doing. It was three of 'em, an older guy and two girls. One girl lost her legs and the other girl lost a chunk of her ass. They jumped off holding hands.

It's really scary sometimes. But we would also hitch sometimes, but hitchhiking could also be scary in another way . . .

I asked her if she would ever do it again and she said: I don't know. I think I would like to do it up to Portland in the summer. It can be kind of rough. I think I like that about it, but when I was doing it, part of me sort of felt like, in a way, you kind of have to have no sense of your own mortality. And now I'm a much more fearful person. It becomes really stressful to figure out, where do we go, what do we do? There were points when we were not talking at all. It's just so miserable. But it's so nice when you're finally out of the city limits and you can smoke or drink whiskey or whatever.

5.

So even brave Dolores was done. Steve thought he might quit before he reached sixty. Pittsburgh Ed allowed that it was getting difficult; he never expressed enthusiasm to me about trainhopping except when referring to *back then.*

As for me, where was I going, and where was *here*? That was as mysterious to me as the shine of spittle on the track of an old trestle bridge. As Kerouac's guru Dean Moriarty says: *We give and take and go in the incredible complicated sweetness zigzagging every side.* A man whom I know only via telephone told me about catching a hot shot out of Weed and passing through Oregon in *two or three hours*; he and his comrades had caught out in three-piece suits, and by the time they got to Seattle they *looked like chimney sweeps* and their hair was stiff with tar. I love the awe of the track's wide nights, and the laughter, even, but my laughs are mainly retrospective, for I was never as quick nor as merry as the road-riders of London and Kerouac. My aspirations ride the long string of colored containers rushing north beneath the misty mountains, cars green, grey and vermillion. Who am I? Long after I thought this book was finished I had a dream that my father and I caught out together, in matching shirts, stowing away in the guts of a freightcar whose angles, complexities and mechanical whirligigs had never before existed; we had to crawl over some sheetmetal ductwork which bent under our weight, and my father warned me to be careful; once we had crossed it safely, he promised to draw me a diagram of whatever lay beneath it. When we had gotten to Everywhere, we were walking down the tracks and I saw that my shirt was utterly black with railroad grime while his was nearly immaculate, because he was my father, my guide and protector who knew everything and could scarcely be touched by death. I woke up almost in tears. So who is he and what can I do and where should I be? The mountains of Glacier, Montana, are going lavender in the rain that strikes these boxcars which I have not yet ridden past the verdi-gris ripples and rapids of glacier rivers.

6.

Jim's lodge dated back to 1920. The grand whitewashed main building had an American flag and a huge fireplace. The apple trees were golden-leaved in that season and there were berry bushes everywhere. The river was the same clear brown as my lost sweetheart's eyes. On the far bank, just below the evergreens that were receding into fog, a freight train was coming through.

Steve caught another trout the morning we left. He always let them go. I stood here wondering if I had reached Cold Mountain. Where is Cold Mountain, anyway? Isn't it for the best if I can never be sure I've found it? Thoreau one last time: *How can he remember well his ignorance — which his growth requires — who has so often to use his knowledge?*

chapter twelve

EXPLODING OFF THE WALL

From our boxcar, kind, chubby, tough-as-nails old Steve stares into the darkness of this unknown world, with one hand in his pocket and the other on the open door, while Brian half-smiles at me with his usual sweetness; on another occasion Ira squints and grimaces into the lens of my camera with all the agonized acceptance of our crucified God, with a string of Burlington Northern cars frozen behind him; God he might have been, but not Christ; he is Mercury; and if you try to nail a globule of that tricky metal to a cross, the globule will submit, then ooze away. Rest in peace, you restless!

Sometimes when I ride toward Everywhere, I believe in Cold Mountain. My anticipations then are as substantial as the rolled bales of hay I see in Montana when the geese are swooping around river-islands; and in Great Falls a swollenfaced Indian woman gives me hope that I will soon be kissing Trudy's or Prudy's lips, maybe even right here at the Lucky Nickel Casino; then the blonde plains are going north and Trudy waits just beyond a low blue horizon, the sky dark and heavy over everything.

At other times I am in pain, and all I can think is: *I've got to get out of here. I've got to get out of here.*

What will happen when I finally reach Everywhere? The longer I live, the closer I get. Looking for Prudy or Trudy, who if I followed her all the way to Norway would call herself Trude, I discover a freight train lovingly detailed on the wall of the gutted room in the abandoned motel, soon to be torn down utterly, in Salton City, California. The dark-windowed locomotive is sinister, the train seemingly about to explode off the wall, leap through the air, and shatter into a shower of red-hot shrapnel.

Trains cross the continent in a swirl of dust and thunder . . .

THOMAS WOLFE, "No Door" (before 1940)

SOURCES

EPIGRAPH: — "They said they would rather be outlaws a year..." — Mark Twain, *Mississippi Writings* (New York: Library of America, 1982), p. 63 *(Tom Sawyer,* orig. pub. 1876).

chapter one A SHORT ESSAY ON FREIGHT TRAINS

4 Rousseau, 1754: "It is thus with man..." — Jean-Jacques Rousseau, *A Discourse on the Origin of Inequality, A Discourse on Political Economy, The Social Contract,* trans. G. D. H. Cole (Chicago: Encyclopaedia Britannica, Inc., Great Books ser. [bound with Montesquieu], no. 38, 1952; var. dates for originals), p. 337, *On the Origin of Inequality* (1754).

8 Footnote on train tunnels — Information from Eddy Joe Cotton, *Hobo: A Young Man's Thoughts on Trains and Tramping in America* (New York: Three Rivers Press [Crown Publishing Group, Random House, 2002]), pp. 155–56.

24ff. Montana hobo interviews, train scenes, etc. — Notebooks, 1998.

27 Footnote on "monicas" — Jack London, *Novels and Social Writings* (New York: Library of America, 1982), p. 257 *(The Road,* orig. pub. 1907).

29 Havre: "This had been a hobo stop during the Depression" — Information from Errol Lincoln Uys, *Riding the Rails: Teenagers on the Move During the Great Depression* (New York: Routledge, 2003), p. 183.

30 Farmers — My fact checker, the perfect Miriam Markowitz, has commanded me to omit the apostrophe after this word.

31 "A very dangerous group of people..." — B. J. Koho, Calibre Press Street Survival Newsline No. 196 (Saturday, August 23, 1997), Newsline@ calibrepress.com, p. 1 ("Killer Train Gang a Growing Threat").

33 Footnote: Pittsburgh Ed — Interviewed near the Loaves and Fishes homeless shelter, Sacramento, Halloween 2006.

36 The spokesman in Fort Worth, Texas — Jim Sabourin, spokesman, Burlington Northern, POB 961057, Fort Worth, TX 76161.

50 Lukács's aphorism — Georg Lukács, *History and Class Consciousness: Studies in Marxist Dialectics,* trans. Rodney Livingstone (Cambridge, Massachusetts: The MIT Press, 1971; trans. from rev. German ed. of 1968; orig. German ed. wr. 1922), p. 263 ("Legality and Illegality").

50 Footnote on the "romanticism of illegality" — Ibid., p. 256.

chapter two SO QUIET AND SMOOTH AND LOVELY

51ff. Extracts from *Life on the Mississippi* (orig. pub. 1883) — Twain, *Mississippi Writings,* pp. 523, 560, 474, 271–73, 381, 283.

54 "I reckon I might say they swum by . . ." — Ibid., p. 740. (*Adventures of Huckleberry Finn,* pub. 1885).

chapter three A TAWNY COYOTE LOOKED AT US

58 "Somewhere along the line I knew there'd be girls . . ." — Jack Kerouac, *On the Road* (New York: Penguin Books, 1981; orig. pub. 1957), p.14.

60 Footnote: "To escape a brush with danger . . ." — Jake Macwilliamson, unpublished ms., "To Missouri: 08 09–22 93," which he photocopied for me in 2006; p. xxv.

62 Kerouac's view of blanks shot off in Cheyenne — Ibid., p. 34. In his day, Cheyenne Frontier Days was called Wild West Week.

63 Arvel Peterson's advice — Uys, p. 84.

63 Counterpart advice in Kerouac, *On the Road* — Op. cit., p. 147.

63 Pittsburgh Ed — Interviewed near the Loaves and Fishes homeless shelter, Sacramento, Halloween 2006.

66 "There are some towns that one must always go through softly . . ." — London, p. 303 *(The Road,* orig. pub. 1907).

66 Cheyenne yard bulls during the Depression —Uys, pp. 117–18. In those years a boy named Weaver Dial was trying to catch out of the Cheyenne yard when three bulls, one on the catwalk and the other two on the tracks on either side, forced everybody off. He hopped another frieght, and when they came into Nebraska the three bulls reappeared, undressed the riders at gunpoint, and took half of each person's cash. Donald Kopecky was the youth who saw a twelve-year-old get clubbed by a Cheyenne bull until his eye popped out of the socket.

67 "The constables are horstile . . ." — London, p. 279.

67 Depression location of Cheyenne's hobo jungle — *Sister of the Road: The*

Autobiography of Boxcar Bertha, as Told to Dr. Ben Reitman (Oakland: AK Press / Nabat, 2002; orig. ed. 1937), p. 166.

70 "One never knows..." — London, p. 207.

72 "Each time we crossed into another state, I felt like the early explorers." — Uys, p. 112 (George Rex).

72 "People ask the way to Cold Mountain..." — *The Collected Songs of Cold Mountain,* trans. Red Pine (Port Townsend, Washington: Copper Canyon Press, 1983; orig. poems late 8th cent.?), song 16 (very freely "retranslated" by WTV).

73 Footnote: "Wyoming, I had decided, looked like a fairly crappy state..." — Macwilliamson ms., p. vi.

74 Footnote about tracks drawing the lightning — Jim Tully, *Beggars of Life: A Hobo Autobiography* (Oakland: AK Press / Nabat, 2004; orig. ed. 1924), p. 49.

75 "My way entered Thunder-house..." — Stephen Owen, ed. and trans., *An Anthology of Chinese Literature: Beginnings to 1911* (New York: W. W. Norton & Co., 1996), p. 183 (Sia-ma Xiang-ru, 2nd cent. BC, "The Great One"); "retranslated" by WTV.

76 Jack London in Rawlins — Op. cit., 267.

77 "...Reawaken, and keep ourselves awake..." — Henry D. Thoreau, *The Illustrated Walden, with Photographs from the Gleason Collection,* ed. J. Lyndon Shanley (Princeton: Princeton University Press, 1973), p. 90.

79 "...This whole trip was fucken nuts..." — Ukla's journal, 1993. This was the same trip described by Jake Macwilliamson's ms. The journal is spiral-bound, with unnumbered pp. This excerpt is from 3 consecutive pp., the first one commencing the entry for August 13.

81 The tale of Phoebe Eaton Dehart — Uys, pp. 92–93, 96.

82 "I never had anything but trouble at Ogden..." — Charles Elmer Fox, *Tales of an American Hobo* (Iowa City: University of Iowa Press, 1989), p. 121.

83 Rail connection between Reno and Ogden — London, p. 262.

84 Pittsburgh Ed — Interviewed near the Loaves and Fishes homeless shelter, Sacramento, Halloween 2006.

86 "...A shit hole..." — Cotton, p. 166.

89 "...The men look like Elmers..." — Ukla's journal, August 13, 1973.

chapter four I THINK WE'RE IN SWITZERLAND, CAT

95 Footnote: "Bairns, you needna learn your lessons..." — John Muir, *Nature Writings* (New York: Library of America, Literary Classics of the United States, 1997), p. 30 (*The Story of My Boyhood and Youth,* 1913).

95   Extracts from *The Dharma Bums*—Jack Kerouac, *The Dharma Bums* (New York: Penguin Classics Deluxe Edition, 2006; orig. ed. 1958). Cold Mountain is also mentioned on pp. 77, 159 and 185.

96   "Hoboing is a lonely business . . ." — Uys, pp. 128–29 (René Champion).

97   The tale of Guitar Whitey — Ibid., pp. 267–68 (Robert Symmonds).

97   Footnote: ". . . Far more vicious than during the Great Depression . . ." — Dale Maharidge, with photographs by Michael Williamson, *The Last Great American Hobo* (Rocklin, California: Prima Publishing, 1993), pp. 40–41.

97   ". . . Huge gaping emptiness and joy . . ." — *The Complete Short Stories of Thomas Wolfe,* ed. Francis E. Skipp (New York: Scribner's, 1987; orig. stories bef. 1940), p. 22 ("The Train and the City").

98   Footnote: "The great and final wild uninhibited . . ." — Ibid., p. 284.

98   ". . . Shattered . . . in the realization that we had never dared to play music . . ." — Kerouac, *On the Road,* p. 270.

98   Footnote: Another hobo's desire to murder Tully —Fox, p. 7.

99   "The imaginative young vagabond . . ." — Tully, p. 167. In another place (p. 92), Tully compares a locomotive whistle to the light that lures a moth.

99   "I wanted to get to Mexico. That was it." — Cotton, p. xxviii.

99   Bill's story — Interview in the Loaves and Fishes homeless shelter's Friendship Park, Sacramento, Halloween, 2006.

99   Pittsburgh Ed's story — Interview near Loaves and Fishes, Halloween, 2006.

100   The friend of a friend who got "ambushed with rocks" — Kevin X., telephone interview, December 2006.

100   "Did we get where we were going? . . ." — Jake Macwilliamson, follow-up interview by author, September 2006.

101   Nick Adams's black eye — *The Complete Short Stories of Ernest Hemingway: The Finca Vigía Edition* (New York: Charles Scribner's Sons, 1987), p. 97 ("The Battler").

101   "The one I had seen was so long . . ." — Ernest Hemingway, *A Farewell to Arms* (New York: Macmillan Publishing Co. / A Charles Scribner's Sons Book / Hudson River Editions, 1988; orig. pub. 1929), pp. 228–29.

101   "I lay and listened to the rain . . ." — Ibid., p. 230.

102   "You were out of it now . . ." — Ibid., p. 232.

102   "I lay and thought where we would go . . ." — Loc. cit.

103   "We had to board this train or give up . . ." — Macwilliamson ms., p. iii.

103   "I think we're in Switzerland, Cat." — Hemingway, *A Farewell to Arms,* p. 276.

103 "I tied the boat and held my hand down to Catherine..." — Ibid., p. 277.

104 "Never mind, darling..." — Ibid., pp. 278–79.

105 "I'm not scared, Nickie..." — Hemingway, *Complete Short Stories,* p. 516 ("The Last Good Country").

113 "You should have been an Indian, he thought...." — Ibid., p. 532.

114 Incidents in Nome, Alaska — From notebooks, 2000.

115 Alabama, could "put his spirit under things..." — Cotton, p. 31.

116 The Indians "were hoboing before hoboing was hoboing..." — Ibid., p. 242.

116 "Now if he could still feel all of that trail on bare feet." — Hemingway, *Complete Short Stories,* p. 532 ("Fathers and Sons").

116 "But there was still much forest left then, virgin forest." — Loc. cit.

chapter five BACK THEN

117 Pittsburgh Ed — Interviewed near the Loaves and Fishes homeless shelter, Sacramento, Halloween 2006.

117 Old slogans for the Chicago Great Western and the Illinois Central — Jim Boyd, *The American Freight Train* (Osceola, Wisconsin: MBI Publishing Co. / Andover Publications, 2001), p. 99.

chapter six I'VE GOT TO GET OUT OF HERE

120 "There was absolutely nothing for us in Spokane." — Uys, p. 140 (Tiny Boland).

121 "But I just want to get out." — Macwilliamson, p. xxix.

121 "Who wants Dos Passos' old camera eye?..." — Jack Kerouac, *Windblown World: The Journals of Jack Kerouac 1947–1954,* ed. Douglas Brinkey (New York: Viking, 2004), p. 252 (entry for Nov. 30, 1949).

124 "...The sudden feeling of release and freedom when the last caboose whipped past." — Wolfe, p. 22 ("The Train and the City").

chapter seven DIESEL VENUS

125 "There are two things that put a man on a train..." — Cotton, p. 56.

127 "We'd had food, drink..." — Macwilliamson ms.,, p. iii.

127 "The few times we saw chicks..." — Ibid., p. xv.

127 "...fantasizing of being picked up by an RV motor home..." — Ukla's journal, unnumbered p., entry for August 14, 1993.

127 The hobo who pimped out his wife — Uys, p. 242 (Chester Smith).

128   Tale of the engineer and the waving women — Wolfe, pp. 271–73 ("The Far and the Near").

129   "Like most men, they idealized women too much . . ." — Tully, p. 74.

129   The one-armed hobo who longed for the lovely girl he had when he was in the Philippines — Op. cit., pp. 36–37.

129   The "lovely woman" who gave $10 to Jake Macwilliamson and his friends — Macwilliamson ms., p. xxvii.

132   Dolores — Interviewed at the Cafe Espresso Metro coffee shop in Sacramento, November 2006. She was introduced to me by her friend who worked at a nearby grocery store. The friend was also present.

chapter eight A STICK OF DYNAMITE

142   Accident in reefer car — Uys, p. 105 (Manuel Krupin).

142   Girl's memory of brutal bulls — Ibid., p. 117 (Margaret Dehn).

143   The U. P. spokesman — Mike Furtney, phone interview, *ca.* 1998.

chapter nine A COLD SUN CRAWLED SILENTLY

151   "On the west side of the river . . ." — From notebook, 1997.

chapter ten GRAINER ASTRONOMY

156   ". . . to every man the right to live . . ." — Wolfe, p. 484 ("The Promise of America").

165   Hobo densities in Jack London's time — London, p. 205.

165   Hobo densities in *On the Road* — Op. cit., pp. 87–88.

173   "Kerouac wrote that in Cold Mountain's poems the fog never departs . . ." — *The Dharma Bums,* p. 177.

174   ". . . and upon that track rolled the rearward portion of our supernaturally long train." — This was a profound experience, perhaps a manifestation of the Worm Ouroboros. I am not the only one who was affected. After writing about it, I heard from Kevin X., whom I had asked for special memories of trainhopping. He replied: "One of the trains I was on was about three miles long, and I could see it way up ahead of me . . ."

chapter eleven LOST AND FOUND

177   "It's like my friends, who work forty years at the same fucking job . . ." — Maharidge and Williamson, p. 17.

177   "If you have any enterprise before you . . ." — Thoreau, p. 23

178   "We lacked that something in us . . ." — Maharidge and Williamson, p. 73.

178 "... A curious nobility ..." — Wolfe, p. 275 ("The Bums at Sunset").

178 "... Foul, filthy, wretched ..." — Ibid., pp. 231–32 ("The Face of the War").

178 "You were always with people on the trains ..." — Uys, p. 188 (James San Jule).

179 "Well, I guess you can ride, Bo ..." — London, p. 216.

180 "Why should they eat their sixty acres ..." — Thoreau, p. 5. Or, as Charles Elmer Fox put it more specifically (p. 19): "In the past twenty-five years or so you can't do much of anything without getting someone's permission."

180 Description of the Illinois Central caboose — After a photograph in Boyd, p. 151.

181 "Such luxury for a group of poor old hobos." — Macwilliamson ms., p. xii.

181 The hobo who guided and bullied — Ibid., p. xxi.

185 "We give and take and go ..." — Kerouac, *On the Road,* p. 115.

185 The "man whom I know only via telephone" — Kevin X., interviewed by telephone, December 2006.

186 *"How can he remember well his ignorance ..."* — Thoreau, p. 6.

189 Ending epigraph: "Trains cross the continent in a swirl of dust and thunder ..." — Wolfe, p. 82 ("No Door"). My copy-editor notes that although it is not known exactly when "No Door" was written, a Thomas Wolfe bibliography from the North Carolina Historical Society lists its publication from 1933.

ACKNOWLEDGMENTS

Steve Jones, Brian Woods, Mike Pulley, Lizzy Kate Gray and Scott Gregory all either caught out with me or sincerely tried to. Meagan Atiyeh and I got kicked out of a trainyard together. Micheline Marcom kept me company on a couple of train track safaris and once found herself beside me in the middle of a trestle bridge when a train appeared behind us.

Paula Keyth introduced me to Jake Macwilliamson, who drank with me, answered questions on two occasions and lent me his trainhopping accounts and journals, together with the journal of his friend Ukla, whom I also thank. As the reader already knows, I cited both of their accounts on more than one occasion. Paula also put me in touch with her friend Kevin X., to whom this book is happily indebted, and, through Kevin, with the legendary Sporticus.

Anna, the cheese slinger at a local market, introduced me to "Dolores," whose stories grace this book.

Peter Maravelis gave me the phone number of Eddy Joe Cotton, whom I wished to ask a couple of questions about the experiences he recounts in his memoir *Hobo.* We exchanged messages but never quite connected. Peter, thank you anyway.

Ross Peterson inspired me with a trainhopping tale or two, and promised to come rescue me if I got stranded anywhere near Salt Lake.

Paul Slovak gave me that copy of *The Dharma Bums.*

Miriam Markowitz, the fact checker at *Harper's,* caught a couple of embarrassing errors (for instance, the Roseville yard is not the longest in the West, and it is six miles long, not seven). I am sheepishly grateful to her. Roger Hodge, her boss, actually gave me money for my trainhopping, and who can beat that?

I also thank Dan Halpern, my editor; Millicent Bennett, his assistant; and Susan Golomb, my agent. Casey Panell and Casey Ferguson, who both work at Susan's office, were extremely kind and helpful. My father figures in these pages, and I often benefit from his bravery and honesty when I try to do my best on the rails. My copy-editor, Don Kennison, rescued me from several more embarrassing errors. I truly appreciate it.

The following persons refused to return phone calls for this book: George Slaats, Union Pacific Railroad; Michelle (last name unknown), the public information officer for the Sacramento police department; and Detective Mike Quankenbush of the Salem, Oregon, police department.

PHOTOGRAPHS

1. American flag design on Union Pacific locomotive, Marysville, California, 2006.

Yard to Yard

2. Graffiti'd NO TRESPASSING sign in the Salt Lake yard, 2006.
3. EUGENE BOUND, Missoula, Montana, 1998.
4. Boxcar door, rainy dawn, Roseville yard, 2006.
5. Boxcar door, early morning, brief stop between San Luis Obispo and Oakland, 2005.
6. Boxcar door, desert dawn, Wyoming-Idaho border, 2006.
7. Rushing grainer car, morning, above the Feather River Canyon, 2006.
8. Birds over tracks, Roseville yard, 1998.

A Few Adventures of Steve Jones

9. Steve Jones, superhopper: Portrait on a chemical car deck not far out of Cheyenne, 2006.

10. Steve trying to figure out just where in the hell in Wyoming we might be, 2006.

11. Steve gazing out of our boxcar door somewhere in Idaho, 2006.

12. Steve and Brian looking out of our boxcar door not far out of San Luis Obispo, three in the morning, 2005.

13. Steve and Brian, same time and place.

14. Steve preparing to abandon our boxcar, rainy evening near Wheatland, California, 2006.

15. Steve with the trout he's just hooked at Jim's place in Dunsmuir, 2006.

Trains, Tracks and Scenes

16. Tracks and ballast, Marysville, California, 2006.

17. Levee tracks at Binney Junction, Marysville, 2006.

18. Shadow of trestle bridge in water, Portland, Oregon, 2006.

19. Trestle bridge, dusk, Sacramento, 1997.

20. Locomotive headlights, Spokane yard, 1998.

21. Train panorama from overpass, San Luis Obispo, 2005.

22. Overpass, Sacramento, 1997. It was here that I tried to catch out with George (see # 35) and got busted.

23. Trainman catching onto locomotive 1308, Spokane, 1998.

24. Locomotive 4580, Marysville, 2006.

25. Marysville house seen through coupling, 2006.

26. Range and cattle seen from chemical car deck, Wyoming, 2006.

27. Rear of train in desertscape seen from boxcar door, Idaho, 2006.

28. Grainer speeding through snowy forest, near Willow Junction, California, 2006.

29. Hobo waiting room, Salt Lake yard, 2006.

Hobos, a Cop and Three *Citizens*

30. Hobo with lowered head, Roseville, 1998.

31. Hobo who liked to talk about the serial killer of hobos called Side-track, Roseville, 1997.

32. Hobo by the side of the freeway, Missoula, Montana, 1998.

33. Ira, near Cut Bank, Montana.

34. Ira again, same time and place.

35. George and his puppy on train overpass, Sacramento, 1997.

36. Sojourner camped near his dog's grave, Sacramento, 1998.

37. Jake Macwilliamson and two of his children, Portland, 2006.

38. Badger, Cheyenne, 2006.

39. Sheldon, Salt Lake, 2006.

40. Pittsburgh Ed, Sacramento, 2006.

41. Officer Herrin, Roseville, 1997.

42. Waitress at the Luxury Diner, Cheyenne, 2006.

43. Barmaid and cook at Mom and Dad's, Soda Springs, Idaho, 2006.

Homage to Diesel Venus

44. Buttocks, G-string and headless torso on the wall of our boxcar from San Luis Obispo to Oakland, 2005.

45. Stylized breasts and vulva on the wall of our boxcar from Rawlins to Soda Springs, 2006.

46. Breasts and vulva labeled "Red River Valley," boxcar, 2005.

47. Moniker of the Short Punk Girlz, boxcar, Spokane yard, 1998.

48. Moniker of Yellow Rose, underpass, Cheyenne, 2006.

A Stick of Dynamite

49. "Niggers are fucking rednecks now." Sacramento, 1998.
50. "Fuck the system; kill the Jews." Salt Lake, 2006.
51. "Go home, wet back!" Cheyenne, 2006.
52. "Fight one on one, punk!" Cheyenne, 2006.
53. "Homosexual ass fuckin'." Sacramento, 1998.
54. "No bums, no queers." Sacramento, 1998.
55. "I hate my life." Spokane, 2006.

Hobo Beds

56. Bed by the tracks, Sacramento, 1997.
57. Bed in the trees, Sacramento, 1997.
58. Bed and hobo stove near the tracks, Sacramento, 1997.
59. Couple sleeping on the far side of a wall, San Diego, 2004.
60. Sleeper by the tracks, Portland, 2006.

Exploding Off the Wall

61. Graveyard tracks, Marysville, 2006.
62. Roseville yard, night, 2005.
63. "Always a good time," Cheyenne, 2006.
64. Lovejoy columns before their removal, Portland yard, 1998.
65. Graffito of train exploding off a wall, abandoned motel (since torn down), Salton City, California, 1996.

3.

5.

7.

8.

9.

10.

13.

19.

27.

29.

30.

31.

32.

33.

35.

36.

37.

42.

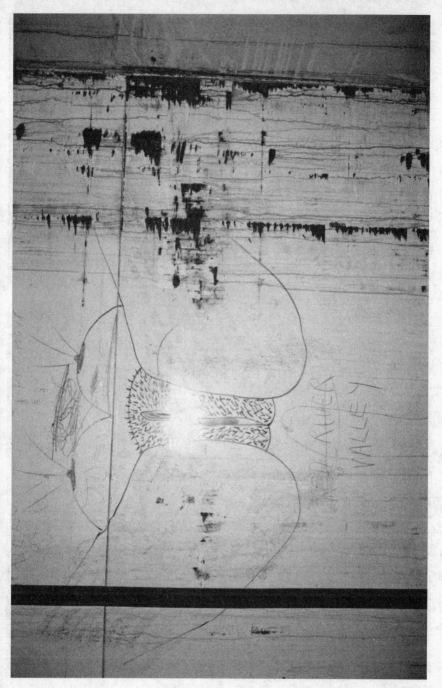

47.

48.

49.

51.

54.

56.

57.

59.

61.

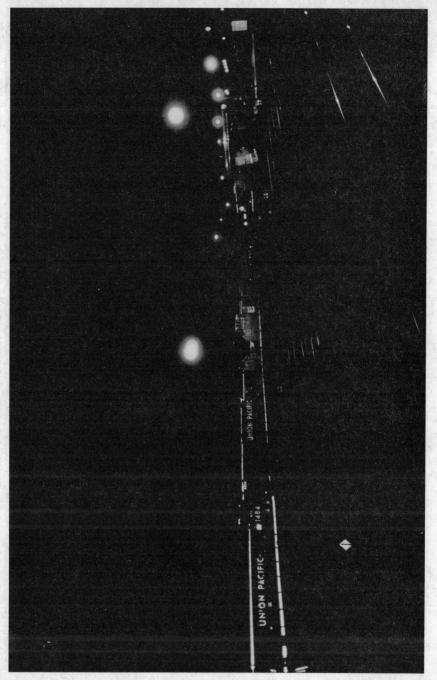

62.

63.

65.